Humble
Pie
and
Cold
Turkey

Humble Pie
and
Cold Turkey

**ENGLISH EXPRESSIONS
AND THEIR ORIGINS**

CAROLINE TAGGART

Michael O'Mara Books Limited

This paperback edition first published in 2023

First published in Great Britain in 2021 by
Michael O'Mara Books Limited
9 Lion Yard
Tremadoc Road
London SW4 7NQ

A CIP catalogue record for this book is available from the British Library.

This product is made of material from well-managed, FSC®-certified forests and other
controlled sources. The manufacturing processes conform to the environmental
regulations of the country of origin.

ISBN: 978-1-78929-514-6 in paperback print format
ISBN: 978-1-78929-347-0 in ebook format

1 2 3 4 5 6 7 8 9 10

Designed and typeset by Claire Cater
Cover and interior icons from shutterstock.com

Printed and bound by CPI Group (UK) Ltd, Croydon, CR0 4YY

www.mombooks.com

MIX
Paper | Supporting
responsible forestry
FSC® C171272
www.fsc.org

Contents

Introduction

The English language is endlessly fascinating. Or endlessly baffling, depending on how you want to look at it. There are so many expressions that, taken literally, make no sense. Why should something *out of left field* be unexpected and odd? Why should being *on a high horse* make you arrogant? What is particularly *plain* about a *pikestaff*? Why should *blue blood* suggest aristocracy and *a red-letter day* be exciting?

The answers to these questions can be found in fields as wide-ranging as baseball and medieval jousting. Other expressions in this book are taken from sailing ships and military formations, Ancient Greek government and nineteenth-century theatre, fashions at royal palaces and the interpretation of dreams in the Bible. Oh, and Shakespeare, of course: you can't get away from him. He gave us a ***wild-goose chase*** and ***a sea change***, ***short shrift*** and ***fast and loose***, to pick just four.

Individual words can have intriguing histories, too. The first people to be ***ostracized*** were Ancient Athenians being exiled from their city; early ***blackmail*** was practised in the Scottish borders; ***undertakers*** were for three hundred years merely helpers, those who ***undertook*** certain tasks, before becoming specifically those who dealt with the dead. And the American equivalent, ***mortician***, was deliberately coined because undertakers in the USA didn't like being called undertakers.

Like ***ostracism*** and ***blackmail***, words and expressions can endure hundreds of years after the events and customs that spawned them have ceased to exist. It's probably two millennia since anyone sent a goat into the desert to carry away the sins of the local populace, but a human ***scapegoat*** can still take the blame for someone else's actions. A certain murderous military order that hasn't existed since the thirteenth century has left us with both the concept of an ***assassin*** and the word to describe one.

Sadly, many of the stories told about the origins of words and expressions can't be verified; some of the best are unlikely to be true. But if the story is interesting enough, I've included it anyway: you can always tell people that you ***heard it through*** *the grapevine* – an expression that itself has sparked more than one explanation. Just don't allow yourself to be *taken aback* if someone challenges you; if you do, *your goose* – and mine – *may be cooked*.

But enough of this *eating humble pie*. Most of what follows is worthy of *a seal of approval* or *a thumbs-up*. Let's not *rest on our laurels*, though: instead, let's *galvanize ourselves into action* and start *talking turkey*.

CHAPTER 1

Big Wigs and Festive Boards

If charity begins at home (as some say it does), let's pretend vocabulary starts there too. Here are a few examples of words we've drawn from our houses and homes.

Smart fifteenth- and sixteenth-century houses were built with the top storey larger than the ground floor, producing an overhang known as a *jetty*. Like the *jetty* that sticks out into a harbour and was originally designed to protect it, it can be traced back to the French word *jeter*, to throw, and is related to *jut*. So the defining feature of any jetty is that it *juts out* from something. The *jet of steam* that emerges from a boiling kettle and the *jet engine* that powers *jet aircraft* come from the same source – they're all to do with some sense of throwing or thrusting. But the sticking out part of the house pre-dates the other meanings by a hundred years and the jet engine didn't make it into the newspapers until the 1940s.

Similar in concept to the jetty are the **eaves**, the part of a roof that projects beyond the side of a building. (Strictly speaking the eaves *is* this part of the roof, because the Old English singular ended in *s* and people came to assume that it was a plural when it wasn't. No matter – in modern English eaves are generally considered plural.) The place underneath the eaves, outside the building, onto which rainwater was likely to drip, was called, as early as the ninth century, the **eavesdrip** or, later, the **eavesdrop**. So a person who stood there was in a good position to overhear anything that was being said inside – though they ran the risk of getting wet if it happened to be raining. Shakespeare uses the idea in *Richard III*, when the king, haunted by ghosts on the eve of the Battle of Bosworth, wants to check on the loyalty of his troops:

> *Under our tents I'll play the eaves-dropper,*
> *To see if any mean to shrink from me.*

Richard's tents probably didn't have eaves – tents don't, as a rule – but the concept of listening in was well established by the time Shakespeare was writing about them.

Inside the house...

...we have some intriguing names for furniture. An **ottoman**, a rather old-fashioned word for a padded seat, was so called because it was covered with **ottoman leather**, named after the Turkish dynasty that ruled a substantial empire from the thirteenth to the early twentieth centuries. A **divan** is Turkish, too, and has a colourful ancestry: when the word first appeared, in the sixteenth century, it meant a council presided over by the sultan. From there it developed into the chamber in which the council met, then a more relaxed sort of chamber, with one side open to provide an attractive view. By the beginning of the eighteenth century a divan was an item of furniture, presumably originally found in such a chamber and described by a British traveller in the Middle East as *a sort of low stages* [sic]*...elevated about sixteen or eighteen inches or more, above the floor... Upon these the Turks eat, sleep, smoke, receive visits, say their prayers, etc.*

The Turkish court must have enjoyed its comforts: we owe it the word **sofa**, too. The English clergyman Samuel Purchas, in a 1625 collection of travellers' tales, describes *a Sofa spread with very sumptuous Carpets of Gold, and of crimson Velvet embroidered with very costly Pearls.* Sadly, that level of luxury doesn't always feature in a modern three-piece suite.

Another pleasure of modern living we owe to the Ottoman Turks is the *tulip*, introduced by them to Western Europe in the sixteenth century. The name comes from a corruption of the word for *turban*, which the open petals of the flower were said to resemble.

One of the many meanings of *board* is a table, especially one spread with food (*the festive board* is a rather dated way of describing a celebratory meal; *bed and board* means you get meals as well as somewhere to sleep). *Above board*, meaning open and honest, comes from this sense. If you're playing cards and your hands and cards are visible above the table, you're unlikely to be cheating by, say, pulling another card out of your sleeve. Nowadays, there doesn't need to be a table involved. In modern life, it's likely to be your accounts rather than your cards that need to be *above board*, so that your auditors rather than your fellow gamblers can see that you aren't doing anything that you shouldn't be.

Another example of this sort of board is a *cup-board*, which was, in the fourteenth century, a table or dresser on which cups were arranged. In a wealthy home the cups would probably be of silver and accompanied by plates, goblets and the like. The piece of furniture on which they sat – called a *sideboard* if it was placed at the *side* of a room, against the wall, rather than in the centre – might well have drawers, shelves or what we would today call cupboards, but for the first 150 years or so of the word's life, a cup-board's principal purpose was ostentatious display rather than storage. At a banquet given by Edward VI in 1551 in honour of the Dowager Queen of Scotland, the young king recorded that *there were two cupboards brought in, one of gold four tiers high, another of solid silver six tiers high*. It's safe to assume that these were designed to impress.

From head to toe

Personal adornment has also enriched our vocabulary, even when the styles it refers to have gone out of fashion. In the seventeenth and eighteenth centuries, a smartly turned-out gentleman would wear a long wig decorated with powder – look at portraits of Charles II or Samuel Pepys to get the idea. Formal dress in British law courts mimics this to this day, with judges wearing long wigs for ceremonial occasions. Thus someone wearing a *big wig* came to be called a *bigwig* – a powerful or important person – and the term endured after fashions had changed and men reverted to displaying their own hair. The American equivalent *big shot* seems to be connected with *shot* meaning a person who *shoots*: a *good shot*, *dead shot* or *big shot* was someone to be reckoned with, whether or not they wore a wig. Such people could also be described as the *top brass*, a term that originated in nineteenth-century military circles in the USA, because of the shiny metal badges and other insignia worn by senior officers.

The best-quality wigs were made from human hair (Pepys didn't dare to wear his new one, bought at the time of the Great Plague, in case it had been made with hair cut from a victim of the disease and still carried the infection). Cheaper versions were made of horsehair or goat hair, but all were curled so that they resembled a sheep's woolly fleece. So to **pull the wool over someone's eyes** meant not to jerk a loosely fitting jumper upwards over their face, but to jerk their wig downwards over their eyes. You could then rob them, lead them astray or otherwise bamboozle them. The figurative expression retains that last sense of to deceive or mislead: *They completely pulled the wool over my eyes – I had no idea what they were up to.*

In the days when women of all ages had long hair, one of the signs of a girl growing up was that she **put up** her hair: either rolling it into a bun or chignon, or covering it with a cap. It was seen as undignified, even improper, to wear it any other way. **Letting your hair down** was something you did only in private, when it needed to be brushed, washed or (if you were rich and fashionable enough to employ a hairdresser) restyled. By the mid-nineteenth century, therefore, **to let your hair down** had come to mean to behave in a relaxed or indiscreet manner, and you didn't have to be female or have long tresses to do it: *After a few drinks everyone began to let their hair down and the gossip got more and more salacious.*

By the way, in the fifteenth century, if you loosened your hair you were described as **dishevelled** (from the French **cheveux**, hair); it wasn't until the seventeenth that **dishevelled** came to mean generally untidy, from head to foot.

And speaking of feet, it was only towards the end of the eighteenth century that shoemakers began making boots or shoes specific to the right or left foot; before that, the two items that made up a pair would be exactly the same. So if one was uncomfortable, you could try it on the other foot to see if it fitted better. Hence the idea that **the boot is on the other foot**, meaning that there has been a change in circumstances. When the idiom was first used, it was often **the boot is on the other leg**: men's boots, after all, came a good way up the calf or even over the knee. Today's usage need not have anything to do with footwear: *I used always to be desperate for money, but now the boot's on the other foot: the rest of the family come to me when they need a loan.*

The idea of differentiating between a left and a right shoe might once have been described as **new-fangled**. It's one of the many words we owe to Shakespeare, though in his day it wasn't necessarily an insult: he uses it in a sonnet to describe clothes that have been **new-fangled ill** – that is, badly refurbished. The **fang** part is nothing to do with teeth; it comes from an old Germanic word meaning to grasp or take hold of.

No smoke without fire?

Modern **perfumes**, of course, are intended to smell enticing, but an earlier, more practical use is suggested by the word's etymology: it comes from the Latin for **to smoke** and is related to **fume** and **fumigate**. In the sixteenth century, perfumes were substances such as incense which gave off a pleasant smell when burned and were used not to enhance a person's attraction but to clear lingering unpleasantnesses from a room. They could also be inhaled as a medical treatment: a 1578 *New Herball* – a guide to medicinal plants – advised that *the parfume of the dryed leaues* [of a plant called foalfoot] *layde vpon quicke coles, taken into the mouth through the pipe of a funnel…helpeth suche as are troubled with the shortnesse of winde*. A rare example of smoking apparently improving your breathing.

Speaking of smoking, many cities across the world in the nineteenth century boasted opium dens where you could – in the classier establishments – relax on a couch (or perhaps a SOFA or an OTTOMAN, see page 13) and smoke opium through a long pipe held over an oil lamp. As the drug warmed up you inhaled the vapours and gave yourself up to the pleasures of hallucinatory dreams. If the Sherlock Holmes stories of Arthur Conan Doyle are to be believed, London's docklands abounded with opium dens, but there was no shortage of them in the

United States, from San Francisco to New York and various metropolises in between. It was there, in the late nineteenth century, that a metaphorical *pipe dream* came to mean a particularly unrealistic ambition, nothing to do with opium: *I've always wanted to go on the stage, but if I want to earn a decent living I'm afraid that's just a pipe dream.*

Something else that might have made you think you were dreaming when you first saw it was the *bikini*, a word that must boast one of the most bizarre of all etymologies. Bikini Atoll is a group of islands in the Marshall Islands of the Pacific, and it was here that the USA carried out nuclear weapons testing in the 1940s and '50s. Shortly after the first test, in 1946, French designer Louis Réard adopted the name to launch his revealing two-piece swimsuit to a flabbergasted world, hoping that it would cause a similar explosive reaction.

Bikini is a Micronesian word meaning 'coconut place': it has nothing to do with the Latin prefix *bi-* meaning 'two' (*biennial, biped, bifocal*, etc.). So it was linguistically absurd to call an even more revealing one-piece swimsuit a *monokini*, using the Greek *mono-*, meaning 'one' (as in *monologue* or *monopoly*). But the designer Rudi Gernreich, who invented the costume and coined the word in the 1960s, almost certainly knew that and equally certainly didn't care. Like Réard, he was out to create a fashion explosion.

Keeping in touch

Back in the days when no one had a telephone in the house, let alone in their handbag or pocket, you had to rely on less sophisticated forms of communication. Something that was *within cry* or, in the language of some Australian aboriginals, *within cooee* was close enough for someone to hear you if you called – an easy distance, in other words. *A far cry* was further than that, a long way. It's an expression that may have been coined by the Scottish novelist Sir Walter Scott, who was a great one for reviving or making up elements of rural Scots dialect. In his *Legend of Montrose*, set in the mid-seventeenth century, he writes:

> *One of the Campbells replied, 'It is a far cry to*
> *Lochow'; a proverbial expression of the tribe,*
> *meaning that their ancient hereditary domains*
> *lay beyond the reach of an invading enemy.*

Whether or not this was a Campbell proverb in the 1640s is open to question – it might be a product of Scott's imagination – but his is certainly the Oxford English Dictionary's first recorded use. Nowadays *a far cry* doesn't have to refer to physical distance: *in 1920s New York it was a far cry from the slums of the Bowery to the wealth of the Upper East Side* is also true, although the distance involved is only a few miles.

CHAPTER 2

Scapegoats and White Elephants

Moving on from furniture, clothes and accessories we come to food, and to the plants and animals required to produce it. But first, a word of warning: from ancient times to the present day, you've had to know which plants were safe to consume. On the face of it, this should require you *to know your onions*, but that expression, dating from the early twentieth century and meaning to be well-informed or experienced about something, probably derives from a person's name rather than the vegetable. The person in question may be an English lexicographer called Charles Onions, or it may be one S. G. Onions, who issued dummy coins to nineteenth-century schoolchildren to help them understand the complicated pounds, shillings and pence system. Or it may not. The OED says that the origin of *to know your onions* is unknown and, given that Charles Onions was once that dictionary's editor, you'd think that, if he had been involved, they'd have been aware of it.

Season to taste

The symptoms of poisoning through consuming certain plants, notably some of the hemlock family that did away with the Greek philosopher Socrates, include what is known as a *rictus grin*, a sustained spasm of the facial muscles. The Latin name for this condition is *Risus sardonicus*, because it was originally believed to be caused by a plant grown in Sardinia. Early uses of the adjective *sardonic* – from the seventeenth century – were always associated with smiling or laughing: making a bitter, mocking look or sound, with no amusement or pleasure in it. Since the nineteenth century you can also make *a sardonic remark* or possess *a sardonic sense of humour* – a cynical one, more likely to point out failings than recognize good qualities. A person may also have *a sardonic look in their eye*, suggesting that they don't believe a word you're saying but are amused by your nerve. For obvious reasons, tourist sites promoting Mediterranean holidays prefer the adjective *Sardinian*, which doesn't imply a connection with either poisonous plants or cynicism.

Rue isn't poisonous but it is bitter-tasting. It was a common culinary herb in Roman times (and in later centuries was considered to protect against snake bites, black magic, poisonous toadstools, the plague – you name it, rue dealt with it). Writing in the first century AD, Pliny the Elder quotes this recipe from a hundred years earlier:

> *Take two dried walnuts, two figs and twenty leaves of rue; pound them all together, with the addition of a grain of salt; if a person takes this mixture fasting, he will be proof against all poisons for that day.*

It's hard to imagine that a grain of salt could counterbalance the taste of so much rue if walnuts and figs couldn't, but presumably it rendered the whole concoction more palatable. Today if you take something *with a grain (or pinch) of salt*, you are treating it with scepticism – a very different matter from making it easier to swallow. The first recorded instance of this sense is in a seventeenth-century biblical commentary by a cleric called John Trapp. Citing an earlier commentator's interpretation of a tricky verse in the Book of Revelation, he observes, 'But this is to be taken with a grain of salt' – which may not explain the origin of the expression but does suggest that the honourable tradition of one academic slagging off another goes back at least four hundred years.

Salt also acts as a preservative, enabling you to keep meat fresh through the long winter months, so if you *salt something away*

(nowadays more likely to be money than food), you are saving it for a rainy day, and also allowing supplies to build up over time: *For years he's been salting away a few pounds a week, so he must have quite a nest egg by now.* (We'll come back to NEST EGGS a bit later – see page 50.)

If salt helps an unpleasant medicine or doctrine go down more easily, *rubbing salt in the wound* has the opposite effect. It was once believed to be cleansing and healing; today it simply hurts, particularly in an emotional sense: *It was bad enough when he broke up with me; going out with my flatmate was rubbing salt in the wound.* This is a surprisingly recent idiom, first recorded by the OED in Australia in the 1940s.

On the other hand, being *the salt of the earth* goes back two thousand years and is the reverse of hurtful: it means you're a decent person, adding a desirable savour to life. In the course of his Sermon on the Mount, reported in the Gospel of Matthew, Jesus tells his followers *Ye are the salt of the earth* and, moments later, *Ye are the light of the world*, so it was obviously quite a compliment. In the same verse, by the way, he advises against *hiding your light under a bushel* (a bushel being a container large enough to hold a bushel of corn or other dry food – 8 gallons or about 36 litres): instead, put it on a candlestick so that it lights the whole house. You should also, Jesus continues, *let your light so shine before men, that they may see your good*

works. Don't be overly modest, is the message: it's all right to be proud of your own achievements. Particularly if you are the salt of the earth.

Being worth your salt or ***earning your salt*** is also a good thing. The word ***salary*** comes from the Latin for salt, which was once an expensive commodity, so if you earned your salt, you were doing well. It's perhaps not as good as being ***worth your weight in gold***, a concept that has been around since the English language was in its infancy, but it's still impressive.

The same is true if ***you cut the mustard***: you're making the grade, performing to the required standard. It's not clear why this should be. ***As keen as mustard***, yes – it shows verve, enthusiasm, perking things up the way mustard perks up the comparative blandness of a ham sandwich. But even when you're harvesting mustard, you don't cut it: you simply rub the seedpods through your fingers and release the seeds. A bit of a mystery, that one, but it's been around, originally in the USA, since the end of the nineteenth century, so the fact that it's a mystery doesn't seem to bother the people who use it.

Speaking of ham…

…if you were a mediocre jazz musician, actor or other performer, you might once have been dismissed as a ***hamfatter***: some trombonists are said to have kept ham fat in their pockets to grease the slides of their instruments and make them easier to play. It can't have been very hygienic, but presumably that was less important than sounding like a virtuoso. There was also, in the late nineteenth century, a minstrel song called 'The Ham-Fat Man' (sung in those days by a white man with his face blackened and therefore likely to be unconvincing and/or overacted). Shortened to *ham*, the word moved away from jazz to refer to an amateurish over-actor, who could be relied upon to *ham up* an emotional scene; from there it became an amateur or enthusiast of any kind, particularly a *radio ham*.

A ham, of course, is quite a large joint of meat – it's a pig's entire thigh – so to be *ham-fisted* or *ham-handed* is to have large, clumsy hands or to be clumsy or insensitive generally: *He made a ham-fisted attempt to apologize, which upset everyone even more.*

Not far removed from ham is *bacon*, a cured form of pig meat and once upon a time also the fresh meat, which we now call pork. At traditional country fairs, chasing a greased pig was a popular event – again, hygiene doesn't seem to have been in the forefront of anyone's mind. Whoever caught the pig took it home and was said *to bring home the bacon*; hence the more generic meaning of achieving success, often in a financial sense. If you *save your bacon*, though, it's your own flesh you're worrying about – you may be escaping from physical harm or from something that would be damaging to your reputation.

There's sometimes even the implication that you might be doing this by that narrowest of margins, *the skin of your teeth*.

No one is sure where the word *piggyback* – carried on the shoulders of someone else – came from. Early forms of the same expression are *pick pack* and *pick back*, and a secondary meaning of *pick* is to toss with a pitchfork, so what has ended up sounding like a pig is more likely to have originated as tossing something on to your back and/or carrying it like a backpack. It's all a bit confused; the only thing that seems certain is that it's nothing to do with pigs.

If a pig is large, an ox or a bull is even larger, so *to beef something up* is to make it stronger or, if it's an idea, to expand it, to fill in the details. Yet *to beef about* something is to complain about it – perhaps to kick and struggle like the animal in a steer-wrestling contest, a rodeo event that became popular towards the end of the nineteenth century, about the same time as the expression first appeared. The more modern *have beef with someone* is presumably a variation on this theme.

Continuing up the size scale, Asian elephants have been used for thousands of years to pull logs and other heavy burdens, to transport people and to carry them into battle. In Siam (now

Thailand) in the nineteenth century the rare white variety of elephant was revered and not permitted to work. The story goes that the King of Siam would make a present of a white elephant to a courtier who displeased him, so that the man was burdened with the expense of its upkeep but not allowed to make it do anything useful or profitable. *A white elephant* soon came to mean any useless and expensive possession: *Having a stately home in the family may sound impressive, but it's a complete white elephant if you can't afford to heat it or repair the roof.*

Herds and flocks

To go back to more conventional farm animals, the general perception of sheep is that they gather in flocks and are not very bright, following any individual who takes the initiative. When it comes to *separating the sheep from the goats*, though, the sheep are the favoured ones. The idea is another from the New Testament Gospel of Matthew and refers to the time of the Last Judgement, when, basically, every human is going to be rewarded or punished for all eternity, depending on how they have behaved so far:

> *Before [Jesus] shall be gathered all nations; and he shall separate them one from another, as a shepherd divideth his sheep from the goats; And he shall set the sheep on his right hand, but the goats on his left.*

Jesus then proceeds to reward the sheep – his loyal followers – and curses the goats – those who have rejected him – sending them off into everlasting fire prepared by the devil. Modern usage, dating from the early twentieth century, is less drastic: **separating the sheep from the goats** may be achieved on a training course, say, that shows who is potential management material, without the non-achievers being condemned to perpetual torment.

The original **scapegoat** had more luck than its New Testament relatives. It appears in another biblical story, this time in the Old Testament book of Leviticus. On the Day of Atonement, two goats are chosen. One is sacrificed, while the other is allowed to escape (or **'scape**) into the wilderness, but not before the priest has confessed over its head all the sins of the Children of Israel, which the goat then symbolically carries away with it. Today, and since the early nineteenth century, a scapegoat is less fortunate: it continues to take the blame for others' misdeeds but there's no modern equivalent of running away into the wilderness. You stay where you are and you carry the can: *Somebody had to be seen to take responsibility, so she became the scapegoat and lost her job.*

If sheep are considered stupid, lambs are known for their gentleness and innocence: someone going **like a lamb to the slaughter** has no idea that they are walking into danger or that they're about to get the sack or the telling off of their life. In the days when animals were slaughtered to appease the gods – particularly the rather harsh Old Testament God of the Jews and the Christians – lambs were popular sacrificial victims. In the Book of Genesis, God tests Abraham's loyalty by ordering him to sacrifice his son Isaac. Father and son go off, ostensibly to worship together, and Isaac innocently asks, 'Where is the lamb for the burnt offering?' Abraham thinks he is sparing his son's feelings when he replies that God will provide, but in fact that is precisely what happens, Abraham is deemed to have passed the test and Isaac is saved.

Later in the Old Testament, the Book of Isaiah predicts the coming of the Messiah and the way that He will suffer in order to take away the sins of the world:

> *He was oppressed and He was afflicted, yet He opened not His mouth; He was led as a lamb to the slaughter, and as a sheep before its shearers is silent, so He opened not His mouth.*

The prophet Jeremiah is even more explicit:

> *I was like a lamb or an ox that is brought to the slaughter; and I knew not that they had devised devices against me.*

It was a popular concept, is what I'm saying.

Even if they weren't being led to the slaughter, flocks of sheep or goats were always vulnerable to predators, as is illustrated by one of the fables of the Greek slave Aesop, who probably lived in the sixth century BC. It concerns a bored shepherd boy who thought it would be fun to shout for help, pretending that a wolf was attacking his sheep. All the villagers came running to the rescue and the boy had a good laugh at their expense. Unfortunately he did this again and again, until the villagers stopped believing him, with the result that when a wolf did appear they left him and his sheep to perish. *To cry wolf*, therefore, came to mean to raise a false alarm and to risk not being believed even when you tell the truth.

That bored shepherd boy – or his employer – probably marked his sheep so that he could differentiate members of his flock from anyone else's. At some time between Aesop's era and our own, a shepherd might have done this with tar, a usefully sticky substance that doesn't wash off in the rain. You'd think that identifying members of the same group would be a good thing, but being *tarred with the same brush* (or, in earlier usage, *with the same stick*) seems always to have been pejorative. Walter Scott, early in the nineteenth century, uses it with reference to *rank Jacobites and papists*, meaning that the members of these two troublemaking groups are as bad as each other. While that usage is still current, there may also now be a suggestion that you are being unjust: *You mustn't*

tar all the committee with the same brush: the treasurer is quite efficient.

To go back to Aesop for a moment, his tale of **the dog in the manger** is brief and to the point. One translation reads, in its entirety:

> A dog lay in a manger, and by his growling and snapping prevented the oxen from eating the hay which had been placed for them. 'What a selfish dog!' said one of them to his companions. 'He cannot eat the hay himself, and yet refuses to allow those to eat who can.'

Thus **a dog in the manger** became anyone who doesn't want something until you try to take it away from them: *Don't be such a dog in the manger – you never wear that necklace, so why not let me borrow it?*

Birds of a feather

So if sheep are stupid and lambs are timid, chickens are cowardly, hence **chicken-hearted** (found in the early seventeenth century) and **to chicken out** of something that would require courage (twentieth century and originally American). In the game of **chicken** (also American and twentieth century) the idea is to drive cars at each other without breaking or swerving, or to cross a busy road while ignoring fast-moving traffic: the winner is the last one to *chicken out*, though the down side is that they are likely to be dead or at least badly hurt. If you cut a hen's head off its reflexes allow it to carry on moving for a short time, though of course there is little point in this. Since the nineteenth century, if a person *runs around like a headless chicken*, they're engaging in frenetic but futile activity: *The closer we got to the deadline, the more we ran around like headless chickens.*

The anonymous sixteenth-century pamphleteer who came up with the expression *he wouldn't say boo to a goose*, meaning he's very nervous, he won't speak up for himself, obviously thought that geese were shy and retiring, which surely suggests that he had never met one. Less open to question is the idea that geese fly in formation. That, believe it or not, seems to be the origin of the expression *a wild-goose chase*. It now means a waste of time, looking for something that you are never going to find, possibly because it doesn't exist. But in the seventeenth century, before horse racing as we know it today came into being, *a wild-goose chase* was a form of racing in which one horse had to follow the course taken by another, both accurately and a prescribed distance behind, like geese in flight. Shakespeare uses the expression in *Romeo and Juliet*, but it's in a scene full of banter between Romeo and his friend Mercutio and it seems to refer to a form of sport that actually involved a goose. The idiomatic meaning, involving neither horses nor geese, came along a few decades later and is still with us: *He deliberately gave false information to send the police on a wild-goose chase.*

The most useful goose in history, or at least in Classical literature, was the one that laid golden eggs. It first appears in another of Aesop's fables, and was obviously a valuable possession. True, it laid only one egg a day, but that's not a bad rate of productivity for a goose. Its owners, assuming that their goose had a lump of gold inside, killed it in order to access this wealth, but discovered that its insides were no different from those of any other goose. So they had lost a steady income stream through wanting to get rich quick. There's a moral there, but then it wouldn't be a fable if there wasn't.

If you'd prefer to get rich steadily and reliably rather than overnight, you can turn to a more modern expression: the ***cash cow***, which dates only from the 1970s. A cow, of course, is something you can milk, and a cash cow can be milked without too much effort or investment to produce a dependable income or profits: *Office rentals were the company's cash cow, providing a steady turnover as the private property market rose and fell.*

Shakespeare seems to have invented the idea of **the milk of human kindness**, meaning compassion, decent human feelings. 'Yet do I fear thy nature,' muses Lady Macbeth about her husband when she learns of the witches' prophecy that he will become king. 'It is too full o' th' milk of human kindness to catch the nearest way.' She means that Macbeth won't want to speed things along by murdering the present king. Shakespeare, like most of his contemporaries, would have been brought up on the medieval medical tradition of the four 'humours' (see page 143), bodily fluids including blood and phlegm which were associated with certain types of personality. It may have seemed reasonable to imagine a fifth humour, milk, the gentle nourishment given to babies, that produced kindness. Or, being the great phrasemaker that he was, he may simply have recognized a good line when it came to him.

The Promised Land of the Old Testament is described as *flowing with milk and honey*, two commodities likely to be rare and desirable in the desert country of the Middle East, giving us an expression that can be used to indicate abundance of any kind. But for real luxury, of course, you want cream. **La crème de la crème**, the cream of the cream or best of the best, was coined in the mid-nineteenth century and combines the two highly desirable characteristics of alliteration and sophisticated-sounding French. As for **the cream of the crop**, which means much the same thing, it's a bit of a mystery. In the OED's earliest recorded use (1850s), the 'crop' in question is cotton cloth, not renowned for its creaminess. The most likely explanation is that it was an alliterative improvement on the earlier *pick of the crop*, coined by someone who acknowledged that *la crème du produit agricole* didn't have much of a ring to it.

Going back to geese, there's a lot of speculation about why *to cook someone's goose* should mean to ruin their chances, but none of it is very satisfactory. One story tells of a sixteenth-century king of Sweden who invaded a nearby country (Denmark? Estonia? Opinions vary) with only a small army. As he approached one town he was insulted to see a goose hanging at the gate, apparently to indicate that this was all he'd be able to shoot. He ordered his men to set fire to the town, explaining to the townspeople that he was *cooking their goose*.

There's no convincing evidence that this is true; nor is it likely that the words were spoken on the deathbed of a fifteenth-century Czech theologian called Jan Hus, whose name translates as goose, because the expression isn't recorded in English until the nineteenth century. In 1835 the magazine *The Public Ledger* reported:

> *Because the defendant would not give them facilities for running contraband goods ashore they had threatened to cook his goose for him; in other words, to be revenged.*

So when this was written the expression was new enough or unconventional enough to require an explanation. In Britain at this time goose was most people's bird of choice for Christmas dinner: turkey would become much more popular following the publication of Charles Dickens' *A Christmas Carol* in 1843, though a Christmas goose is the focal point of a Sherlock Holmes story, 'The Blue Carbuncle', published in 1892. A Christmas goose was often ordered specially and killed shortly before the big day; few people could afford to eat it at any other time of year. So perhaps to cook someone's goose for them was to kill it prematurely and spoil their celebration. Or perhaps, as others have suggested, the story is related to the goose that laid the golden egg (page 34), and the point is that once that special creature is killed (and cooked) it is of no further use.

As I said, lots of speculation, no very satisfactory answer.

A sitting duck is easier to pin down. It began as a military term for an unmissable and defenceless target: shooting one is akin to *shooting fish in a barrel*. Both are originally American expressions, from the early part of the twentieth century; *like taking candy from a baby* is slightly earlier and you can't help wondering why the American language needed so many ways to describe doing something that is easy but unfair. To *have all your ducks in a row* is also American but isn't originally to do with poultry: a duck in this context is a short, fat skittle used in bowling. If they are all in a row, they are ready to be bowled at; away from the bowling alley it means you have everything organized, you're in control of whatever situation you might be in: *You'd better get your ducks in a row; someone from head office is coming round this afternoon.*

There's no apparent reason why *a lame duck* should be any more useless or more to be pitied than anything else that can't walk, but the term goes back to the eighteenth century, well before *duck* was used as a casual synonym for *person*, as in *an odd duck* or *a clever duck*. It's also before *duck* came to mean no score in cricket (see page 117). In the 1760s a lame duck was specifically a person who couldn't meet their debts; in John Galsworthy's *The Man of Property* (the first volume of *The Forsyte Saga*, published in 1906 but set in the 1880s), young June Forsyte is *continually taking up with 'lame ducks' of one sort or another* – in Forsyte terms, impractical young men with no money, not good husband material. More recently, American presidents nearing the end of their term of office have been described as *lame ducks* because they aren't able to achieve much in the time remaining to them. But why a duck? Sadly, no one seems to know.

Nor does anyone seem to know how *to talk turkey* (originally *to talk cold turkey*) came to mean to talk frankly. There's an archaic American expression *to say turkey*, or more often *not to say turkey*, not to say a word on a subject: related to not saying boo to a goose, perhaps? So *to talk turkey* is the opposite: it means to get to the point and – to drag in a metaphor that's been in use since the sixteenth century – *to call a spade a spade*. Why coming off drugs just by abruptly stopping and enduring the unpleasant symptoms that follow should be called *cold turkey* is another mystery: maybe it's a reference to talking cold turkey, in the sense of getting on with the process and not trying to avoid the difficulties. All these expressions are originally American, of course, because most things to do with turkey are: the Pilgrim Fathers ate turkey at what is traditionally regarded as the first Thanksgiving, in 1621, simply because it was there and the locals recommended it.

The delightful word *gobbledygook* can also be credited to the turkey: *gobble* – which already existed as a verb meaning to eat quickly and greedily – was co-opted in the eighteenth century to represent the typical sound a turkey makes, the equivalent of a rooster's *cock-a-doodle-doo* or a duck's *quack*. *Gobbledygook* seems to have been coined in the USA during World War Two to designate pretentious and long-winded bureaucratic language, and its invention is credited to a man whose family had already made its mark in the world of words. He was the Texan Senator Maury Maverick, and his grandfather, Samuel Maverick, was the independently minded rancher who insisted on not branding his cattle to show that they belonged to him. Samuel thus gave his name both to an unbranded calf and to a person who refuses to conform to social convention or any party line.

CHAPTER 3

Olive Branches
and Apple Pies

Moving for a moment out of the farmyard into woods and parkland, a healthy squirrel has bright eyes and a bushy tail, so a person who is *bright-eyed and bushy-tailed* is alert, brisk and enthusiastic: as a description of a human being, this is first found in the USA in 1860. Squirrels are also known for their habit of burying nuts in times of plenty so that they can feed themselves during the winter: humans (since the early twentieth century and again originally in the USA) are more likely to *squirrel away* small sums of money which mount up over time (see also SALT SOMETHING AWAY on page 23 and NEST EGG on page 50). Rabbits, on the other hand, are renowned for sexual activity (*at it like rabbits*, *breeding like rabbits*) and for doing everything they do very quickly. It's presumably from this that – as recently as the mid-twentieth century – we took to ***rabbiting on***, talking at speed and at length about nothing in particular.

The one thing a rabbit doesn't do quickly is get out of the way of an approaching car: ***to be caught like a rabbit in the headlights*** is to freeze, to be paralysed by fear or surprise. This needn't be because of the threat of an oncoming vehicle: an embarrassing or unexpected question, or being caught doing something you shouldn't be doing, could have the same effect. Particularly in the US, the animal in question is sometimes a deer rather than a rabbit: it depends on where you live and what, as a night-time motorist, you're most likely to surprise. But the feeling of immobilizing horror is the same.

Not so much a night-time motorist as a night-time hunter might find his dog ***barking up the wrong tree***. Raccoons, pesky things inclined to raid rubbish bins and the like, were commonly hunted in the eighteenth and nineteenth centuries; they're nocturnal, so it made sense to do this at night, and they spend a lot of their time in trees, so it was the role of the 'coon hound' to smell a raccoon out, stand at the bottom of the appropriate tree and bark to indicate where the quarry was. Raccoons aren't stupid, though, and they're agile, so they could easily flit from one tree to the next, leaving the dog nonplussed and doing its barking in the wrong place. By the 1830s the concept was being applied to people who were misdirecting their energies

– originally in the US but it had crossed the Atlantic well before the end of the century: *You're barking up the wrong tree if you think I can help you. I don't have a moment to spare.*

We all know that snails are slow, and that they are capable of retreating into their shells when danger threatens. What may be less well known is that their eyes are set into tentacles that can also be retracted if necessary. Thus **to draw in one's horns** – to become less adamant about something, or to spend less money – is one of the few idioms deriving from the habits of snails. It's found as far back as 1400, an age when people perhaps had more time to stop and observe the mini wonders of nature.

A bit of a problem

It's the Bible that gives us the idea of **a fly in the ointment,** a small imperfection that spoils everything. The Old Testament Book of Ecclesiastes is quite graphic about it:

> *Dead flies cause the ointment of the apothecary to*
> *send forth a stinking savour: so doth a little folly*
> *him that is in reputation for wisdom and honour.*

The nineteenth-century essayist Charles Lamb has moved on

from the literal to the figurative, but he PULLS NO PUNCHES (see page 125) either:

> *A Poor Relation is—the most irrelevant thing in nature…a lion in your path,—a frog in your chamber,—a fly in your ointment.*

To make it sound even more undesirable, **chamber** here means not **bedroom** but **chamber pot** – the 'convenient' receptacle kept in bedrooms in the days before en-suite facilities. Not somewhere you'd choose to find a frog.

Another unwelcome burden – particularly if you have done something that comes back to haunt you – might be **an albatross around your neck**. In Samuel Taylor Coleridge's 1798 poem *The Rime of the Ancient Mariner*, the mariner of the title for no apparent reason shoots an albatross that has been following his ship and has brought it safely through a storm. In maritime tradition, albatrosses are the bringers of good luck and to shoot one is to court disaster. Disaster does indeed strike the ship and the mariner's shipmates hang the dead bird around his neck as a symbol of his guilt. Today **an albatross around your neck** can be anything that stops you making progress, from a property you can't sell to a successful parent whose reputation overshadows yours: *Having a comedian for a father became an albatross around his neck when he wanted to be a serious actor.*

The other thing – nothing to do with birds – that may figuratively hang around a neck as an inescapable burden or duty is a ***millstone***. The origins here are literal: millstones, used to grind grain into flour to make bread, were heavy things; if you got crushed by one you stayed crushed, and if someone hung one round your neck and threw you into deep water, you drowned, simple as that. A figurative millstone, first found in the fifteenth century, can be more or less anything onerous: *My unsuccessful novel was a millstone round my neck when I was looking for a publisher for my memoirs.*

Unground grain was known as grist, so that if something is ***grist to the mill*** it's useful, able to be turned to your advantage: *No experience is wasted on a writer: watching people in the street and eavesdropping in the supermarket are all grist to the mill.*

Being ***put through the mill*** (or ***going through the mill***) may not have been fatal, but you would still emerge exhausted after an illness, say, or a rigorous course of study or period of difficulty. There's a suggestion that you have learned something from the experience, like the wedding guest to whom the Ancient Mariner has told his story: we are told that he goes away 'forlorn' and

> *A sadder and a wiser man*
> *He rose the morrow morn.*

The grain or *corn* that went into a mill was a commonplace, basic thing. Perhaps when the growth of cities and shops allowed city folk to buy their bread ready made, without worrying about what went into it, the ingredient itself came to be regarded as rustic and unsophisticated. Hence, from the 1930s, the use of *corny* to describe something (originally jazz) as unpolished, unoriginal and trite. The OED's first recorded use occurs in the British music magazine *Melody Maker*; in America a decade later *cheesy* was being applied with similar urban snobbery to anything clichéd or in poor taste. Both words could also be used to deplore excessive sentimentality. Oddly, the Yiddish-derived *schmaltzy*, meaning much the same thing, is based on a word for the animal fat used in cooking, and again was first used in the 1930s to disparage a certain sort of music. What popular music of that period had done to provoke all these food-related insults is a matter for speculation.

Something that is *run-of-the-mill* doesn't necessarily come from the sort of mill that grinds grain; it could equally be the product of a sawmill or a paper mill. *The run of the mill* is simply whatever the mill produces, before any selection or quality control has been done. An 1876 report on the productivity of a mineral district in Tennessee gives the exact sense: *Lumber is cheap. Ten dollars per thousand is the price for inch lumber, the run of the mill; $12.50 for choice.* Today, something that is *run-of-the-mill* doesn't need to have been anywhere near a mill or factory, it merely has to be ordinary, unexciting, mediocre: *a run-of-the-mill detective story* has no sensational plot twists, while *a run-of-the-mill restaurant* is unlikely to win Michelin stars.

Time for a little something

It's probably no surprise to learn that the French invented the *restaurant*, a word that originally meant *restorative*, specifically a restorative meat broth or *bouillon*. The 1988 edition of *Larousse Gastronomique*, the bible of all things food-related, explains:

> *In about 1765, a Parisian 'bouillon-seller' named Boulanger wrote on his sign: 'Boulanger sells restoratives fit for the gods', with a motto in dog Latin:* Venite ad me omnes qui stomacho laboretis, et ego restaurabo vos *(Come unto me, all you whose stomachs are aching, and I will restore you). This was the first restaurant in the modern sense of the term.*

The bouillon-seller's name is a pleasing coincidence, as *boulanger* is the French for 'baker'. With any luck, he offered decent bread as an accompaniment to his hearty broth.

The French also invented the **bistro** or **bistrot**, a smaller and less formal version of a restaurant. This name may come from a regional word, perhaps in Occitan, the medieval language of southern France, related to Catalan. Certainly cassoulet, the sausage-and-bean stew often served in early bistros, is an Occitan dish, so perhaps the first bistro owner in Paris was a southerner. There is, however, an alternative explanation; it's disputed but decidedly more exciting. The Russians took control of Paris in 1814, at a late stage in the Napoleonic Wars, and tradition has it that their soldiers, with no time to linger over their meals before going back on duty, demanded to be served **bistro**, which is the Russian for 'quickly'. Experts doubt the truth of this, as the word **bistro** isn't found in French until 1884, but it's one of those stories you'd like to believe.

Like Monsieur Boulanger's establishment, a respectable bistro would be expected to serve decent bread. Most 'bread' expressions, however, refer not specifically to the stuff that you slice and spread butter on but to the broader meaning of food in general, the amount you need to keep you alive. Dating from two thousand years ago, the line from the Christian Lord's Prayer that asks God to **give us this day our daily bread** is simply requesting enough to eat; when, a few decades later, the Latin poet Juvenal wrote that the Roman people had grown so self-indulgent that they weren't interested in their democratic rights but were content with **bread and circuses**, it went without saying that they'd be happier with some salami and a few olives thrown in. Not to mention something in a flagon to wash it down. *To earn your (daily) bread* is to work for a living, and has been for several hundred years, while in Australian or New Zealand slang someone wondering about your line of business might ask *What do you do for a crust? Dough*, the stuff of which bread is made, has been (originally American) slang for money since the mid-nineteenth century, though *bread* has been familiar in that sense only since the 1950s and '60s.

An idiom that, despite appearances, almost certainly *isn't* related to bread is *upper crust*. The widely publicized suggestion that the top part a loaf was reserved for the aristocracy is less probable than the idea that the expression alludes to the layers of the Earth. *Upper crust* was used to mean the surface of the planet as early as 1555, when it referred to a place where rubies were found; in the early nineteenth century it could also be the human head or a hat; and only after that did it become a term for the upper tier of society.

From the earliest times (perhaps the twelfth century in England), markets were strictly regulated and selling poor-quality goods or short measures was heavily punished. Bakers in particular became known for supplying thirteen loaves when twelve were asked for, to be sure of not running into trouble with the authorities. Hence ***a baker's dozen***, meaning thirteen. If a customer suspected he was being cheated he might insist on having the produce weighed. While this was being done, the product could be said to ***hang in the balance***, the ***balance*** being the scales, the device that did the weighing. In other words, the issue was undecided, as it is in a broader sense today: *The election was very close, with the result hanging in the balance until the last vote had been counted.*

I said we'd come back to nest eggs (see page 24). The original ***nest egg*** was literally an egg, real or artificial, that was put into a hen's nest to encourage her to continue laying after you'd collected what she'd produced so far. In use in this sense from at least the fourteenth century, by the seventeenth a nest egg had become a metaphor for a sum of money put aside for future use. Presumably the logic is that the literal nest egg is a small investment that produces a good return (in the form of more and more eggs) over a period of time.

In another of Aesop's stories a hungry fox spies a tempting-looking bunch of grapes hanging on a vine above his head. When he finds that he can't reach them, he goes grumpily away, muttering that they obviously weren't ripe and wouldn't taste sweet. So you may be accused of ***sour grapes*** when you pretend to despise something you can't have.

Sour grapes apart, fruit is generally seen as a good thing: *the fruits of your labours* are the pleasing result of hard work. Plums are particularly desirable: *a plum job* is one that brings authority, prestige, a good salary but not too much aggravation. On the other hand, if you have *a plummy accent*, you talk as if you had *plums in your mouth*: this originally meant you drawled or spoke indistinctly, but came to be associated with the British upper classes (presumably the only ones who could afford plums) and just meant posh, in a pretentious and unpleasant sort of way.

An olive, or at least an olive leaf, has been a symbol of peace since biblical times. When the waters of the Old Testament flood are abating, Noah sends out a dove to see if it can find dry land and it eventually returns with *an olive leaf pluckt off* in its beak. We now normally offer *an olive branch* as a gesture of goodwill or to patch up an argument, but Noah's dove has only a leaf. There may be an overlap with the olive wreath of Ancient Greek times – the goddess Athena presented an olive tree, representing prosperity and peace, to the city of Athens at the time of its foundation. Thereafter, wreaths of olive leaves were worn by various dignitaries and as a sign of victory at the Olympic Games. In Roman times the olive gave way to the laurel (associated with the god Apollo) as the plant of choice for wreaths, worn by victorious military commanders during their triumphant processions. If, having achieved this honour, you never did anything praiseworthy again, you could be described as *resting on your laurels*, looking back complacently at your past accomplishments: *It's no good resting on your laurels – you need to get out and drum up new business*. This dates from the nineteenth century, as does its opposite, **to look to your laurels**, to seek to stay ahead of your rivals by repeating those successes.

From being symbols of peace, **doves** developed into politicians who favour negotiation or conciliation over confrontation and open warfare. It was during the Cuban Missile Crisis of 1962 (one of the many occasions since the end of World War Two when it looked as if another global conflict was on its way) that such people were first described as the opposite of **hawks**, the warmongering element who, according to the Philadelphia *Saturday Evening Post, favored an air strike to eliminate the Cuban missile bases*. Let's bomb them and get it over with, is the hawkish attitude; the doves are happy to spend time trying to save a few lives.

But we were talking about fruit. In early medieval times the apple was a synonym for the pupil of the eye, which was thought to be a solid, spherical body. (It isn't. It's a gap in the iris that lets light through to the retina, but not many people knew that back then.) If you lost the apple from your eye, you'd go blind, so you needed to look after it. Thus **the apple of your eye** was something or someone particularly dear to you, to be supported and nurtured. The idea dates back at least to King Alfred (reigned 871–99), who used an Old English version of the words in his translation of an earlier Latin work. In its current form *the apple of one's eye* was around at the time the King James Bible (1611) was being produced. In Psalm 17, the writer, praying for God's protection, asks Him to *Shew me thy marvellous lovingkindness… Keep me as the apple of thy eye, hide me under the shadow of thy wings.*

As for the idea that apples, or rather apple pies, are orderly or that they make beds that are impossible to get into – that may be a mistake. There is a phenomenon in linguistics called metanalysis, which means, among other things, changing the point where a word should be divided. For example, our word *orange* comes from the Spanish *naranja*, but somebody somewhere misheard *a norange* as *an orange*. *Apron* comes from the French *naperon*, so again what began as *a napron* became *an apron*. The French *nappes pliées* means 'folded linen' and sounds enough like *apple pie* for this to have been applied to a bed that has, as a practical joke, been made up with the sheets folded halfway up.

Or so one story goes. The OED is dismissive of this explanation, pointing out that a *nappe* is a tablecloth rather than any form of bed linen. *Nappes pliées order* as the origin for *apple-pie order*, meaning perfect order, a place for everything and everything in its place, is a bit more plausible but not much. It's probably more sensible to visualize one of those open-faced tarts with slices of apple beautifully and symmetrically arranged and to leave French table linen out of the picture altogether.

The best-known example of metanalysis is perhaps **to eat humble pie**, to apologize or be forced to apologize in a grovelling, humiliating way. The **umbles** were the entrails or offal (the heart, liver, etc.) of an animal, usually a deer: the cheaper, less desirable parts of the animal that would have been eaten by the servants in a great house, while the lord and his family and friends had the venison roasted over a spit in one of those vast fireplaces you see in stately homes. The **umbles** might well have been made into a pie to make them more palatable or to make them go further. But the French word from which the name derives was **nombles**, so what started out as **a nomble pie** drifted to become **an umble pie**. Because it was a **humble** dish, eaten by the lowly members of the household, it became confused with that word, which derives from a completely different source. The result is that, although the literal pie is rarely seen these days, the idiomatic one is always **humble**: *The journalist was forced to eat humble pie when analysis of the statistics exposed a number of inaccuracies in her report.*

Something that **went to the pot** was, in the sixteenth century, chopped up to be added to a stew; within a hundred years or so this had been adapted – with or without the definite article – to mean killed, ruined, figuratively gone to pieces: *Everything in his life has gone to pot since he lost his job.*

Nowadays if you come across **pot luck**, it's likely to be a category in a quiz, one in which any subject may crop up. But in the sixteenth century if you were invited **to take pot luck** at someone's home it meant you took your chances on eating whatever was available, whatever happened to be in the **pot**. **A pot-luck supper** is (particularly in North America) one to which lots of people contribute a dish, without necessarily planning a balanced menu, but you can **take pot luck** in other areas, too: you might go to the cinema because you fancied going out and were happy **to take pot luck** on whatever film happened to be on.

You'd hope that any food that came out of your pot would be hot, but if you wanted it **piping hot**, you should probably have put it in a kettle, so that it made a **piping** sound or whistle when it reached a high enough temperature. This is an image that dates back to Chaucer's *Canterbury Tales* (about 1400), where the Miller's Tale refers to *wafers coming piping hot out of the glede* (coals or embers). Perhaps it wasn't the kettle that whistled: it might have been you when you burned your fingers lifting something out of the fire.

Keeping the fire going was important when this was your only means of heating your home and cooking your food; one way of doing this was to use a substantial **log** at the **back** of the fireplace – one that would keep smouldering and keep the temperature up while smaller pieces of kindling came and went. Such a device was, reasonably enough, called a **back-log**, and the term came in the nineteenth century to mean something in reserve, that could be drawn on in time of need. By way of example, the OED cites this wonderfully cynical line from John Steinbeck's 1952 novel *East of Eden*: *If one is accused of a lie and it turns out to be the truth, there is a backlog that will last a long time and protect a number of untruths.* Steinbeck's liar might have consider that that particular backlog was a good thing; today it is more likely to refer to an accumulation of work that hasn't been done: *So many driving tests had to be cancelled because of the snow that by the time the weather improved there was a six-week backlog.*

Oddly enough, John Steinbeck and *East of Eden* crop up again in the next chapter…

CHAPTER 4

Thumbs Up for the Grass Roots

We owe a lot of the vocabulary of government to the Ancient Greeks, and specifically the Ancient Athenians. They came up with the concept of *democracy* – government by the people – a word that was in use in English by around 1500. They also produced *tyrants* (unelected leaders likely to rule cruelly and oppressively, found in English in the fourteenth century), *aristocracy* (government by the best people, sixteenth century) and a particularly harsh law-maker called *Draco*. Under his system an extraordinary range of crimes, from fraud to stealing a cabbage, could by punished by death; the adjectives *draconic* and *draconian*, derived from his name – which appropriately enough means dragon – came into English from the eighteenth century to mean severe and uncompromising.

In addition, the Athenians had their own way of deciding whether or not to send someone into exile. They wrote their votes on broken pieces of pottery known as **ostracons**. Thus if the vote went against you, you were **ostracized**. The looser version meaning to exclude from any group, to refuse to speak to someone, was with us by the seventeenth century.

We owe the Greeks plenty of cultural terms, too. The philosopher Zeno delivered his lectures in a porch or **stoa**, which gives us the adjectives **stoic** and **stoical**, describing the repression of feelings and patient endurance of adversity that Zeno advocated. And in among the many Greek deities were nine sisters known as the **Muses**, patrons of the arts and inspiration for poets, musicians and the like. The first **museums** were buildings that were sacred to the Muses, set aside for study and research. In fact the very first was not a museum in the modern sense but a library – an extraordinary accumulation of knowledge called the **Mouseion**, part of the Great Library of Alexandria, destroyed by fire in perhaps the first century BC but giving its name to collections of all sorts of objects and information ever since.

One further and perhaps surprising contribution from Greek, nothing to do with government or culture: there was a river in Phrygia, now part of Turkey, which was famous for its slow, winding course. Now called the Menderes, it was once known as the Maiandros, and it is from this river that we get the word *meander*, both as a noun meaning the sort of course the Maiandros followed, and as a verb meaning to follow such a course, whether or not you are a river: *We didn't bother with a map; we just meandered round the town admiring whatever ancient building we happened to find.*

The Ancient Romans' contribution was more focused. In any major Roman town, the *forum*, originally the market place, was also the centre of political, religious and social life. The main Forum in Rome contains the ruins of the Senate House, the Rostrum from which speeches were made (and from which we get the modern term for the dais on which speakers stand), various temples and a couple of triumphal arches. It's because so much of the legal activity of Rome took place in the Forum that the adjective *forensic* (which in its Latin form originally meant simply 'to do with the market') developed, by the seventeenth century, into 'pertaining to the law, used in a law court'. Hence *forensic medicine* (concerned, for example, with the cause of a suspicious death), *forensic evidence* (fingerprints or DNA samples collected at the scene of the crime) and more loosely *forensic detail* (very great detail, on a par with what might be needed in a court of law).

Roman public entertainments often involved a fight to the death between two men: slaves, prisoners of war or volunteers, some of them skilled warriors. Only the ones armed with swords were **gladiators** (from the Latin **gladius**, a sword), though we now tend to use that word more loosely and even applied it to a television game show in which participants undertook a wide range of challenges in which swords were conspicuous by their absence. Back in Rome, when one of the combatants was floored and the other was about to plunge a blade into him, the Emperor or most senior official present indicated with a hand gesture whether or not he was to die: thumb up meant 'He's fought well; spare him'; thumb down meant 'Kill him.' We know this: we saw Joaquin Phoenix do it in Ridley Scott's *Gladiator*, with that evil, vengeful look on his face. It must be true.

But it might not be. The Roman writers are less clear-cut about it than Ridley Scott. The second-century satirist Juvenal, presumably an eyewitness, suggests that it was the *crowd* who dictated the outcome; he uses the words **verso pollice**, 'with thumb turned', to indicate a mob that wanted blood. Other Classical authors refer to the 'hostile thumb', but nobody actually specifies which way it is turned to indicate its hostility. The idea that pointing the thumb *down* condemned the fallen fighter to death was possibly invented, and was certainly popularized, by the nineteenth-century French painter Jean-Léon Gérôme, whose 1872 painting *Pollice Verso* shows the crowd with thumbs firmly turned that way.

What the Romans actually did, therefore, has been lost in the mists of time, but *to give something a thumbs-down* is now to condemn it, without or without an accompanying gesture; *a thumbs-up* is a sign of approval: *The proposal has to go to the next board meeting, but the CEO has given me an unofficial thumbs-up.* A thumbs-up is also, of course, the way to 'like' something on online platforms such as YouTube and to indicate 'Yes, fine, message received and understood' in an SMS. Historical accuracy simply doesn't come into it any more.

Skipping forward to Anglo-Saxon times...

...a *moot* was a meeting, especially of something like a local council or a magistrate's court. It was also the place where the meeting was held. An issue that was put forward for discussion at such a gathering could be described as *a moot point* – a *point* to be raised at a *moot* – and the expression has been used since the sixteenth century to mean something that needs to be debated, that isn't easy to resolve. That's in British English; in North America it's gone one stage further and become something that you can quibble over if you like, but that isn't really worth the effort. You can use it as a verb, too: *I'd like to moot the possibility that...* means much the same as the old marketing cliché *I'd like to run it up the flagpole and see who salutes it* – in other words, I'm just making a suggestion to see what anyone else thinks.

From the twelfth century in England, a *scot-ale* was a festival held by the lord of the manor or other official in order to raise money. *Ale* in this context is an old word for a festival and *scot* has nothing to do with Scotland but was a feudal tax, payable by the rural populace to an overlord. Throughout the Middle Ages you find terms like *Rome-scot* (a church tax payable to the Pope in Rome), *soul-scot* (paid to the church on behalf of a deceased person) and so on. If you *got off scot-free*, you didn't have to pay the tax or, from the sixteenth century, you simply got away with some misdeed without taking the consequences: *They were so sound asleep that the burglar got away scot-free* or *He never puts on weight: he gets away scot-free however much he eats.*

In medieval markets, a young pig was a valuable commodity, to be taken home, fattened up and turned in due course into bacon and ham. Dishonest traders were known to take advantage of naïve purchasers by selling them *a pig in a poke* (a poke being a bag or small sack). This meant that purchasers couldn't inspect the goods, so didn't know what they were getting. By the sixteenth century the expression had moved into broader contexts, so that in 1583 the playwright Robert Greene, in his romance *Mamillia*, was able to make this risqué observation: *He is a fool, they say, that will buy the pig in the poke: or wed a wife without trial.* In the original marketplace context, the most likely substitute for the pig was a cat: easier and cheaper for the seller to get hold of, no use whatever to the buyer. Someone wanting to put a stop to this fraudulent practice could *let the cat out of the bag*, an expression that by the eighteenth century could be applied to revealing any sort of secret, not just a dodgy marketing one: *We'd planned a surprise party, but someone let the cat out of the bag, so it wasn't a surprise at all.*

Once markets became substantial concerns, whole streets would be devoted to a particular type of merchandise. The City of London still has streets called Poultry (meaning 'the street where fowls were sold', which is why it isn't Poultry Street), Bread Street, Milk Street and so on. A table or counter on which such goods were displayed was, in the tenth century, called a *shamble*, from an Old English word meaning a bench. By the fourteenth century this had evolved – it isn't clear why – into something specifically used for meat and thus into a meat market. There are still streets called Shambles, most famously in York but also in other English towns, that were once full of butchers' shops. The meaning continued to develop, though. By the sixteenth century, and now usually with an *s* on the end, a *shambles* was not just a butcher's shop but a slaughterhouse; then it became any scene of carnage: the defining factor was no longer the bench or table, it was the blood. And finally (or finally so far) it backtracked again: from a combination of blood and chaos, it became any sort of chaos, whether tangible or intellectual: *The playground was a shambles after the children's party* or *The government's economic policy is a complete shambles and inflation is rampant.* All that from an innocent word meaning a bench.

Going back to medieval times, by no means everyone could write: it's widely rumoured that even King John (reigned 1199– 1216) couldn't. Whether he could or not, he didn't sign Magna Carta in 1215 – he put his seal to it. This was a device depicting the king on his throne, carrying a sword in one hand and a sceptre in the other, and surrounded by a Latin inscription that translates as 'John, by the grace of God King of England and Lord of Ireland'. Looking like a large coin, just under 10cm/4in in diameter, it was pressed into melted wax; that wax, with its image in place, was then tied to the document with a ribbon. You can still see this on the copy of Magna Carta held by Salisbury Cathedral and on the British Library's website. At the time, sealing was the usual way of ratifying a document – other dignitaries had their own seals, so that the image impressed on the wax was as individual as a signature. Using a device like this would **seal the agreement** or **seal the deal**. The concept endured long after signatures became the norm, so that by the nineteenth century giving something your **seal of approval** had nothing to do with wax, or even necessarily with signing your name: it just meant that you agreed: *There's no point in my saying you shouldn't go to the party if your mother's given it her seal of approval.*

There was a feeling of permanence about sealing a document, though: once the monarch had agreed to your execution, say, there was no going back on it – **your fate was sealed**. There's the same inevitability about this as there is about THE WRITING ON THE WALL (see page 157), though there can be a hint of rather high-flown romance, too: *My fate was sealed from the moment I met her – I knew I'd never look at another woman.*

If your fate was sealed in the sense of your being condemned to death, you were likely to give thought to your immortal soul. In the Catholic faith, you did this by making *shrift*, the act of confessing and receiving absolution. In Shakespeare's *Richard III*, Richard has passed sentence of execution on Lord Hastings and refuses to have dinner until he knows that his enemy is dead. So one of the king's henchmen tells the condemned man to 'make a short shrift' – get on with it, he means, the boss is hungry. Subsequent uses of the expression are less brutal but still not very considerate; they tend to take the form of *giving someone short shrift* – treating them quickly and brusquely, not listening to any ideas they may be putting forward.

From the Church and the Bible...

The Christian Church and its various subdivisions haven't always been tolerant of anyone who doesn't follow their views or their forms of worship precisely. In the days of Protestant supremacy Catholics could be burned at the stake for their beliefs; when the Catholics were in charge Protestants went the same way. There were some unpleasantly inventive forms of torture, too, one of them being **to haul someone over the coals** – hot coals, obviously, otherwise it wouldn't have been painful enough. That form of punishment is no longer with us, but **to be hauled over the coals** still means – and has meant since the eighteenth century – to be severely reprimanded. Now, mercifully, it is usually with harsh words rather than anything more physical. Oddly enough, **heaping coals of fire on someone's head** wasn't a torture: it seems always to have been a metaphor for repaying cruelty or unkindness with good will, making the person on the receiving end feel shame and remorse. The Old Testament Book of Proverbs advises:

> *If thine enemy be hungry, give him bread to eat;*
> *and if he be thirsty, give him water to drink. For*
> *thou shalt heap coals of fire upon his head and*
> *the Lord shall reward thee.*

In the New Testament, St Paul's letter to the Romans says much the same thing and follows it with:

> *Be not overcome of evil,*
> *but overcome evil with good.*

Why this benevolence should take the form of heaping hot coals on someone's head is unclear.

Christian baptism is usually done with water, but there are several references in the New Testament to **baptism with fire** – a form of purification carried out by the Holy Spirit. The term was sometimes applied to martyrs who had been executed by fire for their faith, and later to soldiers whose first experience of battle had exposed them to gunfire. Today **a baptism of fire** is not unlike being **thrown in at the deep end** (a metaphor associated with swimming pools), indicating that your first experience of something is a frightening or challenging one: *I'd never spoken in public before, so having an audience of two thousand people was a baptism of fire.*

On the other hand, for people who believed the right thing (whatever that was), the grace of God guaranteed their salvation – a theological concept called **saving grace**. Since the eighteenth century **a saving grace** needn't have anything to do with life after death or with religion of any kind; it's merely a good quality that makes up for a lot of bad ones: *He's always late and he's always scruffy; his only saving grace is that he apologizes so beautifully.*

Another biblical concept that has stood the test of time is that of the **Good Samaritan,** someone who performs an act of kindness for a stranger. In the Gospel of Luke, Jesus has been instructing his disciples to **love thy neighbour** and is asked, 'Who is my neighbour?' In response, he relates a parable in which:

> *A certain man went down from Jerusalem to Jericho, and fell among thieves, which stripped him of his raiment, and wounded him, and departed, leaving him half dead.*

As the man lies there a priest and a Levite (also a sort of priest) come along, see him and famously ***pass by on the other side***. It's a Samaritan – a person from Samaria, traditionally hostile to the Jews – who takes pity on the wounded man, takes him to an inn and looks after him. The point, of course, is that the two priests should be ashamed of themselves and that the Samaritan, who might have been expected to be unsympathetic, has behaved in a neighbourly fashion. The Samaritans charity, founded in the UK in 1953 to help people in emotional distress, takes its name from the same story.

At the other end of the humanitarian scale is Cain, eldest son of Adam and Eve. Cain kills his brother Abel because he's angry at God preferring Abel's offering to his own. When God asks Cain where Abel is, he replies with the oft-quoted words ***Am I my brother's keeper?*** There's no fooling God, though, and Cain is exiled. In the expression ***to raise Cain***, ***raise*** means to conjure up a spirit and ***to raise Cain*** is to invoke the spirit of Cain, to create a really riotous disturbance: *He raised Cain when the airline refused to upgrade him.* ***To raise hell*** or ***to raise merry hell***, to conjure up the spirit of the devil, means much the same thing.

Cain eventually settles in the *Land of Nod*, which in the Bible is a place name with no particular significance, though it happens to lie to the east of Eden, from which John Steinbeck took the title of his 1952 novel. In the eighteenth century, however, the satirist Jonathan Swift (whom we shall meet later, with a proposal for relieving parents of their superfluous babies, see page 153) gave the Land of Nod a new meaning, appropriating it as a jovial synonym for sleep – the place you go when you *nod off*.

Law and order

One way of preventing people from *raising Cain* is *to read them the riot act*. The Riot Act was passed in Britain in 1715, as a way of quelling civil disorder. The Act made it a felony for a gathering of more than twelve people to refuse to disperse when instructed to do so, having been read the relevant portion of the Act by a lawful authority. *To read someone the riot act* (with no need for the initial capitals) quickly became to tell them to be quiet and behave themselves, or just to scold them severely. There no longer need to be thirteen people involved, either; you can do it to a lone recalcitrant teenager: *My parents always read me the riot act if I'm late coming home.*

The *aftermath* of being read the riot act might be some form of punishment, but from Anglo-Saxon times up to the early twentieth century a *math* was an act of mowing, or the part of a crop that had been mowed. The ***aftermath***, therefore, was a second growth of the same crop, the bit that came along ***after*** the ***math***. From the seventeenth century, this could apply to any happening or state of affairs that resulted from something that had gone before: in the ***aftermath*** of an eclipse, normal daylight might seem dull; the ***aftermath*** of a street party might be a lot of clearing up. Unlike the original ***aftermath***, which was a bonus crop, a modern one tends to be unpleasant.

Before they became associated with politics, ***grass roots*** were just what they sound as if they should be: the roots of a grass plant. Perhaps because grass is widespread, commonplace and generally low-growing, the expression came, in the late nineteenth century, to be used in connection with unpretentious people, the ordinary voters supporting a political party, as opposed to the politicians themselves or the party activists. A politician who campaigned at ***grass-roots level*** would be (or at least trying to appear to be) taking the voters' views into consideration, hoping to appeal to what used, in more sexist times, to be called ***the man in the street***.

On a par with the grass roots of a political party are the ***rank and file***: again, the ordinary voters or unsung party members. This was originally a military expression, dating from the sixteenth century: a ***rank*** was a single line of men standing side by side, while a ***file*** was a line of them one behind the other (it's the same sense as in **walking in single file**). So the **rank and file** were a group of soldiers neatly arranged for a drill or inspection. The idea moved into politics in the early nineteenth century and you now commonly hear of **the rank and file of the electorate** or **rank-and-file Democrats**.

A soap box is something else that started life as precisely what you'd expect: a box in which to keep soap. Quite a lot of soap. It was a wooden case, large and solid enough to stand on if you were going to make a speech without a proper stage to raise you above the heads of your audience. In 1907, the American novelist Jack London wrote in a memoir, *I get up on a soap-box to trot out the particular economic bees that buzz in my bonnet,* and the idea of having a bee in your bonnet very much captures the sense in which the metaphorical soap box is now used. You don't need to stand on a box in the park, or even to stand up at all – you can get on a soap box at a dinner party, without moving from your seat at the table, if what you are doing is ranting on a subject about which you feel strongly and not letting anyone else get a word in.

Not far removed from a soap box – in the sense of something you bang on about – is a **hobby-horse**. In the sixteenth century, this was a term for a child's toy; later it was also the sort of horse found on a merry-go-round at a fair. It's from this last meaning – something on which you go round and round, over and over again – that we get the idea of a **hobby-horse** being an obsession: *It's a hobby-horse of mine that children should eat what their parents eat, not be fobbed off with fish fingers.* **Hobby** is a later variation and over time has lost the sense of excessive enthusiasm; it's now simply a harmless pastime that you enjoy.

A **soap opera** is something else whose connection to soap has become tenuous: it is, of course, a radio or television genre, characterized by melodramatic situations usually in a domestic setting, and takes its name from the fact that early sponsors (in the 1930s) were often soap manufacturers, so advertisements for their products appeared in the breaks. **Opera** was presumably used facetiously, by analogy with the equally tongue-in-cheek **horse opera**, coined ten years earlier to describe a western.

Going back to speech-making, speakers who had omitted to bring a soap box with them might stand on the **stump** of a tree in order to attract attention. Since the mid-nineteenth century in the USA, political candidates or individuals with a cause to plead have gone **on the stump**, originally travelling the country from tree stump to tree stump in order to address whatever audience they could muster. As with soap boxes, actual tree stumps are no longer required, but **on the stump** still carries the image of someone doing the rounds of the small towns in their constituency.

One way of going on the stump is to do **a whistle-stop tour**. Nowadays this tends to suggest that you make only the briefest of visits to a number of places, but originally a *whistle-stop* was the place itself rather than the visit: it meant a small town where the train wouldn't *stop* unless requested to do so by a *whistle*. (This was also just the sort of place where there would be no podium and where a speaker would have to stand on a tree stump or soap box.) The concept of *a whistle-stop tour* as a way for politicians to show their face in as many places as possible emerged in the US after World War Two: the first person recorded as going on one was President Harry Truman, seeking re-election in 1948. It obviously worked: having had an approval rating of only 36 per cent in the spring, he travelled over 35,000 kilometres around the country, making speeches not from a soap box or a stump but from the back of a railway carriage, and addressing literally millions of people; the result was a comfortable victory in November. Nowadays it isn't only politicians who make fleeting visits to a number of venues: *We had only two days in Paris, so we did a whistle-stop tour that took in the Louvre, Notre-Dame, the Eiffel Tower and Montmartre.*

Another convenient way of campaigning used to involve a *bandwagon*. This was originally, as you might guess, a *wagon* that carried the *band* or orchestra as part of a circus. The pioneering showman Phineas T. Barnum, who ran the 'Greatest Show on Earth' in the latter part of the nineteenth century, paraded such a wagon as a way of attracting public attention and the idea soon caught on with politicians, who also used it to draw a crowd. Possibly the first person to employ the idea in a figurative sense was the future President Theodore Roosevelt, reviewing the campaign that had brought him the governorship of New York in 1899: *When I once became sure of one majority they tumbled over each other to get aboard the band wagon.*

He meant, of course, that he garnered more and more supporters when it began to look as if he was going to win. Today *to jump* or *climb on the bandwagon* is to join what looks as if it's going to be the winning side, or to follow a successful trend, in or out of politics: *The original series of* Star Trek *was so successful that other studios were soon jumping on the sci-fi bandwagon.* The idiom has even given rise to a business phenomenon, *the bandwagon effect*, according to which companies issue a product or follow a business model simply because they have seen others doing it.

The demon drink

Producing and selling alcohol has often had political and legal implications. *Moonshine* – illegally distilled liquor – acquired its name because it was usually produced at night, 'by the light of the moon'. Because it was illegal, any trade in it had to be secret too, so a dealer would hide a bottle or flask inside the top of his boots. Such a person became known as a *bootlegger* and his goods as *bootleg liquor*. The term is sometimes used in broader contexts – during World War Two rationing, for instance, you might have got a few ***bootleg sausages*** (more than the system had allocated to you) from a friendly butcher; in the days before streaming you might have acquired ***a bootleg copy*** of an unauthorized music or video recording, with no obligation to hide it in your boots.

During the years of Prohibition in the United States (1920–33) and before that in areas where the sale of alcohol was frowned upon, you had to do your drinking not in a pub or bar but in some discreet back room known as a ***speakeasy***. Here you'd be expected to ***speak*** in an ***easy*** manner – gently, calmly, not getting into an argument and not raising your voice so as to alert the police. An optimistic name for a venue whose whole *raison d'être* was to enable you to drink as much as you could before the place was raided.

The concept of ***teetotalism*** pre-dates Prohibition by almost a hundred years and there are a number of complex explanations for the emergence of the word. It came to prominence after a speech given in Preston, Lancashire, in 1833 by one Richard Turner, whose tombstone credits him with inventing the term. Turner was advocating ***total*** abstinence from alcoholic drinks, whereas some previous temperance movements had avoided only spirits. The ***tee*** is likely to have been added for emphasis – it seems trivial to suggest, as some interpretations have, that

Turner might simply have had a stammer, but we can't know for sure that he didn't. Or, hey, he may have meant, 'That's total with a capital T, guys.' Whatever the reason, the word was used (several times) in the *Preston Temperance Advocate*, a magazine started the following year by someone who had heard Turner's speech, and it rapidly caught on.

From the slate to the computer

If you weren't teetotal, you might run up a weekly or monthly account at your local pub; or, teetotal or not, you might do the same at a shop where you were known. The amount you owed was chalked up on a slate behind the bar or counter. In the days before exercise books (which were, in their turn, in the days before computers), schoolchildren also chalked their sums or their alphabet on pieces of slate. When the classroom exercise was done or the bill paid, a quick rub with a duster or sleeve would ***wipe the slate clean*** and you could start the next class or the next week's drinking ***with a clean slate***. Today a bit of community service or even an abject apology could serve the same purpose: *He did a couple of hours' gardening for me and we decided that that would wipe the slate clean* or *We've agreed to forgive and forget and go forward with a clean slate*.

In some games, chalk was used as a way of scoring, with the marks getting longer with each point scored. To win ***by a*** *long chalk*, therefore, was to score a substantial victory. To do anything else *by a long chalk* is to do it by a great degree, a large margin: *He's not by a long chalk my favourite person* means that I really don't like him at all.

Moving on from slates and chalk, schoolchildren in the nineteenth century learned handwriting and arithmetic from copying letters or sums printed in a *copybook*. By this time they were using simple pens dipped in inkwells, which made it distressingly easy to drop a blob of ink onto your page and thus *to blot your copybook*. More generally, this came to mean to make a mistake or commit a misdeed or indiscretion that spoiled an otherwise clean record: *She blotted her copybook by being late for three meetings in a row*. As an adjective *copybook* can mean perfect, flawless – *a copybook example of a Powerpoint presentation* – but may also suggest a lack of originality – *her letters were full of copybook sentiment, but I don't think she really cared what happened to me*.

Another group under pressure to write cleanly and legibly were the clerks in counting houses, where merchants conducted their business and kept their accounts. Such clerks spent much of their time *posting* entries into ledgers: they copied the details of transactions, which had been recorded on individual pieces of paper, into one large book so that turnover, profit and loss and so on could be calculated. It was important that this information was up to date and it's probably from this use of *post* that we get **to keep someone posted**, to keep them informed of developments. Originally (in the mid-nineteenth century) the usual expression was **posted up**, meaning well-informed. **Posting up** was something you often did to yourself: *The exam is next week, so I have to post up on Einstein's theories.* The **up** has now largely been dropped, and **keeping posted** is something you tend to do to other people: *She promised to text as soon as she arrived, so I'll keep you posted.*

Once we'd moved on from counting houses, we came to rely on computers for our information. In the 1940s, the name **computer** was more often applied to the person doing the calculations than to the calculating machine, but it was the machine that was **in the loop**: performing a set of instructions over and over again (**looping** round to start from the beginning once it reached the end) until some specified condition was met. Only then could it move on to the next function. Presumably the implication was that the machine knew what it was doing, because when, in the 1970s, **in the loop** came to be applied to people, it meant well-informed, often with knowledge that wasn't widely circulated: *I know you can't go to the meeting, but don't worry: I'll keep you in the loop.* In that context, your informant might also bring you **up to speed**, an expression that in the nineteenth and early twentieth centuries was applied only to racehorses or cars, meaning that they were running as fast as you might reasonably expect them to.

Being well-informed is obviously of crucial importance in times of war, which edges us gently towards the next chapter.

CHAPTER 5

Running Amok with the Devil to Pay

An island nation that once boasted the most powerful navy in the world, and that spent much of its history battling with its European neighbours, is bound to have plenty of vocabulary to deal with things military and maritime. There's nothing in that to *take anyone aback*.

In the early eighteenth century, in order to be *taken aback*, you had to be a sailing ship. *Aback* had a complicated definition to do with the position of the sail vis-à-vis the wind, but the point was that it wasn't helpful to a sailing ship trying to go forward. So *to be taken aback* originally meant to be caught with the sail in this position, to be unable to make progress. By the middle of the century, it was being used in the modern figurative sense of being surprised or perplexed: *I was taken aback by his generous offer, because he usually hates paying for anything.*

If the mast of a sailing ship happened to snap, it could easily fall overboard or **go by the board**. An expression dating to the seventeenth century, this was used almost entirely in sailing contexts until the nineteenth. Since then, however, it's been applied to any project or resolution that has been abandoned: *The idea of a new kitchen went by the board when we realized how much it was going to cost* or *My good intentions went by the board when I saw chocolate fudge cake on the menu.*

In the days of wooden ships (before about the 1830s), some of the seams in the planking that ran along the keel were known as the ***devil***. It's not absolutely clear why, but it may have been a jocular nickname given by the men whose duty it was to caulk these seams (to pack them with waterproof material to prevent leakage), indicating that they were hard to reach, so that working on them was difficult. This is the sort of devil you're talking about if you are caught **between the devil and the deep blue sea**. It's like being **between a rock and a hard place** – in an uncomfortable situation, forced to choose between two unpleasant alternatives.

Another term for **to caulk**, specifically when using hot pitch or tar, is **to pay**. It's possible that the expression **there'll be the** *devil to pay*, meaning there'll be trouble, also refers to this sort of devil. Particularly if you use the old-fashioned extended version *the devil to pay and no pitch hot*, this is saying that there is a job to do (paying the devil, to stop the ship sinking) and nothing to do it with (no pitch hot enough), so it's going to end in disaster (the ship will sink).

There's argument about this, though: the expressions *the devil to pay, the devil and all to pay* and sundry variants on the theme date back to the eighteenth century, while the earliest use of the 'no pitch hot' version is mid-nineteenth. It's possible that shipworkers took an existing expression and, again, adapted it jocularly to the tools of their trade. The fact that *there'll be hell to pay* also dates from the eighteenth century lends weight to the idea that these expressions originated with the satanic devil (the one who lives in hell) rather than the maritime one. The idea would then be that, like Faust in the Germanic legend and various plays and operas based on it, you had sold your soul to the devil in exchange for some favour or other and the time had come to honour the debt.

Most other sayings to do with the devil (*better the devil you know than the devil you don't, talk of the devil and he will appear, needs must when the devil drives* and many more) are definitely about the satanic version: not only will he find work for idle hands, but he's no slouch himself when it comes to getting people into trouble. All these maxims date back to the sixteenth century or earlier, when the devil featured strongly in Christian teaching and was a personage to be feared. The Catholic Church once employed a ***devil's advocate***, to present the arguments against a suggestion that seemed to have God on its side, such as beatifying or canonizing someone, or declaring that an unusual occurrence was a miracle. Since the late nineteenth century, the term – usually in the form ***to play devil's advocate*** – has been found in contexts other than the Church one. It can describe anyone who disagrees with a proposition in order to test the strength of the arguments in favour of it, or just to be contrary: *Your father's playing devil's advocate. He doesn't object to you taking a gap year; he just wants to know what you want to do with it.*

Going back to paying, though, there's another meaning in use at sea: ***to pay out*** a rope or cable is to release it gradually. According to a former sailor called Richard Edgcumbe, writing in 1898, a cable was often ***paid out through the nose***, the nose being the bow, the part of the ship that projects at the front as the human nose does on a face. The order was often given to ***pay out handsomely***, where handsomely means in a controlled or appropriate fashion, rather than anything to do with good looks. From releasing a cable handsomely to paying out handsome (or generous or even excessive) sums of money was, according to Mr Edgcumbe, a short step.

It's convoluted but just about plausible. Less likely is the explanation given by Brewer's *Dictionary of Phrase and Fable* and elsewhere, that in ninth-century Ireland the conquering Norsemen imposed a *nose tax*, the equivalent of a poll tax. Anyone defaulting on payment was punished by having their nose slit. The reason this gory story falls down is that in medieval Norse the word *nose* was used as English today uses *head*, as a way of counting people ('per head of the population'). As *poll* in this context also means *head*, a nose tax simply meant that each person (each nose of the population) was charged the same amount. That said, a nose tax could easily have been deemed unfair and excessive – witness the violence that greeted the imposition of a Poll Tax in Britain in 1990. Whatever the reason, *to pay through the nose* had come to mean to pay a high price, to pay above the going rate, by the middle of the seventeenth century. This doesn't necessarily mean you're unhappy about it, though: *I had to pay through the nose to get tickets, but it was worth it to see my team in the final.*

A slight diversion

We seem to have digressed a bit from seafaring. Let's take just one more small detour before getting back to the point. A *sea change* isn't really a sailing expression; in its infancy it simply meant a change brought about by the sea. Shakespeare uses it in *The Tempest*, when the sprite Ariel sings to Ferdinand, telling him (wrongly, as it turns out) that his father has drowned and lies under *full fathom five* (about 9 metres) of water:

> *Nothing of him that doth fade*
> *But doth suffer a sea-change*
> *Into something rich and strange.*

It means that everything about him has changed radically, due to the action of the water. Subsequent uses of the term, well into the twentieth century, continue to refer to this song and to the sea. After that it takes on its own momentum, so that a 1970s Tolkien scholar was able to write (without apparent irony) that, in the sequel to *The Hobbit*, *Middle-earth has undergone a wondrous sea change*.

Getting back to seafaring...

...wooden ships (like many other wooden things) were supported and held together by *beams*, long, thick, straight pieces of wood that ran across them horizontally. If the ship was *on its beam-ends*, it was lying on its side, having capsized and being in imminent danger of sinking. A person, business or project that's *on its beam-ends* has also hit an obstacle, run out of money or encountered some other form of disaster.

One of the ship's beams ran across the middle, at its broadest point, and was used to measure the vessel's width. Thus to describe a person as **broad in the beam** is to say that they have a large posterior, though they are unlikely to thank you for drawing attention to it.

If you're about to run into a storm, you have to **batten down the hatches**. A **batten** is a strip of wood, a number of which would, aboard ship, be attached to a tarpaulin. This was then spread over the **hatchways** that gave access to the lower decks. The tarpaulin was obviously to stop rain drenching everything down below and the battens helped to hold it in place. The expression, dating from the nineteenth century, can now be used in drier contexts. *It's always a bit depressing once the clocks have gone back in the autumn and you batten down the hatches at half-past four* means little more than that it is getting dark by then, so you close the curtains and turn on the lights in preparation for the long evening ahead.

While we're describing parts of a boat, the **gunwale** (pronounced and sometimes written **gunnel**) is the upper edge of the side of the vessel. The **wales** are the planks along the outer timbers and **guns** were placed on the uppermost of them. To be **packed to the gunwales**, therefore, is to be packed absolutely as high as possible, so that nothing else can be crammed in. The expression obviously began with cargo ships, but can now be applied to anything crowded: *The toyshop was packed to the gunwales with the latest* Star Wars *merchandising*

or *At six o'clock the bar is always packed to the gunwales and you wait ages to be served.*

Similar in meaning and also nautical in origin is ***chock-a-block***, packed tight, as full as can be. A ***chock*** is a fitting on a ship's deck through which you can run a rope; a ***block*** is part of a pulley system used in a ship's rigging. Since about 1800 ***chock-a-block*** has meant having the two pulled together as closely as possible. Figuratively (and, since the mid-twentieth century, casually altered to ***chocker***) it can be used with reference to any crowded place: *The club was chock-a-block: there was no room to dance at all.*

Two other things that can happen with sailing ships are ***sailing by***, which means heading into the wind, and ***sailing large***, with the wind behind you. Putting the two together, to sail ***by and large*** is to have a bit of one thing and a bit of the other. So to consider something ***by and large*** is to take an overview, to look at it on the whole, generally speaking: *She went on a bit too long, but by and large it was an impressive speech.* Another term for sailing almost into the wind is ***close to the wind***, which since the mid-nineteenth century has had the added meaning of being close to the edge of acceptable or legal behaviour: *He was sailing close to the wind by 'borrowing' from the petty cash.*

In nautical circles, one of the meanings of ***weather*** is 'on the windward side, on the side from which the weather is coming'. ***To keep a weather eye*** seems never to have been specifically sailors' slang, but has been in use since the early nineteenth century to mean to keep a keen eye on, to keep a look out for something: *He was always eager to improve his investments and kept a weather eye on what the markets were doing.*

Sails and what to do with them

A ship's sails are tied to the mast and raised and lowered by a system of ropes. Obviously it's important to put these in the right order and to tie them in the correct places – you need someone who **knows the ropes** (in order to keep everything **shipshape**). This is probably where the expression, dating from the early nineteenth century and meaning to know how something is done, to understand how a system works, comes from: *It was my first day, so I desperately needed someone to show me the ropes.*

To be **shipshape** – **shaped** in a way appropriate to a **ship** – is to be neatly arranged and in good order. It's been known since the seventeenth century and was applied to things other than ships in the nineteenth; you could now say *We worked hard all winter to make the hotel shipshape for opening in the spring.* For extra emphasis, there's the variant **shipshape and Bristol fashion**, **Bristol fashion** being a later nautical expression meaning much the same thing as **shipshape**. Bristol was a major English port, second only to London in importance, from the late fifteenth century onwards, but the image came into use only in the nineteenth. An 1860s dictionary of nautical terms records that **Bristol fashion**, now rather dated, was popular when the city *was in its palmy commercial days...and its shipping was all in proper good order.*

Sheet is a poetic name for a sail, but more technically the sheet is a rope attached to the lower corner of a sail. If this comes loose, you have **a sheet in** or **to the wind,** which gives the somewhat dated slang expression for slightly drunk. The more familiar **three sheets to the wind** would mean the sails were flapping around all over the place – hence completely and utterly drunk.

The wide variety of names for sails, denoting different sizes, shapes and functions, is beyond the scope of this book. Suffice it to say that one of them is called a **jib**. From the early nineteenth century **the cut of your jib** has meant your general appearance or attitude, whether or not you are a ship or even a sailor. It's most frequently used in the expression **I like the cut of your jib**, meaning I like you, I like your outlook on life and I can probably trust you too.

If you have a boat or ship moored at a dock, you have to untie it to send it on its way. A smaller craft might have been hauled up on to the beach, so that to set it afloat you have **to push the boat** *out*. It may be because helping someone to do this was seen as a friendly and generous thing to do that, in the 1920s or so, ***pushing the boat out*** became naval slang for buying a round of drinks. From there it graduated to any extravagant behaviour, not necessarily involving alcohol: *I've never stayed in a five-star hotel before, so I'm pushing the boat out and buying lots of stylish new clothes.*

Sailors in trouble

The idea of a space being so small that there is ***no room to swing a cat*** may also have seafaring origins. If so, it would be referring to ***the cat-o'-nine-tails***, a whip with nine knotted lashes used as a punishment in the army and navy for two hundred years from the late seventeenth century. On a cramped deck, there might have been no room to carry out the flogging efficiently. Alternatively, the expression can be taken at face value: grab a cat by its tail and see how much room you need in order to swing it satisfactorily. Not much, is what the idiom implies.

A different form of torture that can be blamed on sailors is the ***round-robin letter***. This now usually means those much-reviled summaries of the year sent out in Christmas cards, but in the past a round robin was not a letter *sent* to a lot of people but one *signed* by a lot. It was often some form of protest or request, with the signatures in a circle to disguise the identity of the ringleader who, in a more conventional arrangement, would have signed first. The connection with sailors is that the first recorded instance, dated 1698, occurs in a document issued by the High Court of Admiralty, the body that held jurisdiction over matters maritime; other early examples also suggest a ship's crew protesting to its captain about some grievance. And why **robin**? Well, Brewer's *Dictionary of Phrase and Fable* suggests that it comes from the French **ruban**, meaning ribbon, but it's surely unlikely that a group of disgruntled sailors would bother to tie a petition up with a ribbon. More likely is a connection with Robin as a proper name. This has, over the centuries, been applied to all sorts of things, from the mischievous sprite Robin Goodfellow to the bird that was once known as Robin Redbreast, as if that were a proper name. (The same habit of giving members of the animal kingdom personal names has traditionally led us to talk about Jenny Wren, as if all the members of the eighty-eight species of wren were female; there's more on this theme in connection with Tom, Dick and Harry on page 172.) Over the years a **round robin** has also been the name of various round objects, from a plump American fish to a decorative ruff worn round the neck, so basically anything round can be called a robin and, as with as plain as a pikestaff later in this chapter (see page 101), the appeal of alliteration helps the phrase to catch on.

Whose side are you on?

At sea, when you don't know who else might be sailing by, it's a comfort to know where another ship comes from. Equally, on a battlefield, it's important to be able to identify the people who are on your side. That's where the idea of standards or *colours* came from. Every troop or regiment carried a flag of a recognized colour and design, to act as a rallying point for its members; ships would display a flag that indicated their nationality and allegiance. *To strike the colours* (take these flags down) was a universally recognized sign of surrender, whereas *to nail your colours to the mast* was both to make your allegiance clear and to proclaim your determination to fight on to the bitter end – *to stick to your guns*, to use another military image. Metaphorically speaking, *nailing your colours to the mast* has been around since the early nineteenth century, when it was used of politicians declaring which side they were on in a contentious debate. Even older is the idea of *with flying colours* – if you pass a test *with flying colours*, you pass easily and with distinction; a regiment or ship that kept its colours flying was proudly calling attention to itself and making its identity clear.

In the same vein, a ship may fly a false flag – *sail under false colours* – in order to mislead the enemy and then reveal itself at the last minute; a person who does the same thing has been disguising some disreputable motive or behaviour and now *shows themselves in their true colours*: *He seemed very easy-going until someone contradicted him, but as soon as he was annoyed he showed himself in his true colours.*

On a smaller scale – as an individual rather than a ship – you might show your allegiance by wearing a certain colour of coat or uniform. If you wanted to change sides, you could turn it inside out to disguise its distinguishing features. It can't have been very comfortable, but then being a *turncoat* – a word that dates back to the sixteenth century – probably isn't meant to be.

Violence and mayhem

Moving from battles at sea to those on land, violence and destruction have always been fruitful sources of vocabulary. In Roman times, the Vandals were a Northern European tribe famous for the devastation they left wherever they went, including sacking Rome itself in 455 AD. Next time you see a telephone box that has been *vandalized* – put out of order for the sheer fun of it – you can think of them.

Scattering something to the four winds is of equally devastating origin: it's found in the Old Testament Book of Jeremiah, when God promises to destroy various of the nations surrounding

Israel. In this case He's directing His might against the people of Elam, in modern Iran:

> *Upon Elam will I bring the four winds from the*
> *four quarters of heaven, and will scatter them*
> *toward all those winds.*

He relents a few verses later and thinks that He will instead bring the Elamites back as captives, but the original idea was that they would be dispersed across the globe and thereafter be unable to get together or have any real identity or power. The modern sense of the expression needn't be destructive but still involves dispersal: *Our family scattered to the four winds after the war, so we probably have cousins in Australia and Canada that we know nothing about.*

The Elamites were great archers, as were the Parthians, another ancient people whose territory lay within modern Iran. The Parthians' trick in battle was to ride away as if retreating, draw their enemy from cover and then twist round in the saddle and fire off their arrows. This tactic became known as *a Parthian shot*, a term that still describes a cutting remark made as you leave the room, giving your hearer no chance to reply. Such a remark is often also called *a parting shot*, perhaps through confusion with the word Parthian, but also because it's a perfectly reasonable thing to call it – a *shot* fired off, by a bow or a sharp tongue, when you're about to *depart*.

If twisting round in the saddle is too sophisticated for your battle plan, you might prefer to come racing down the hill towards your enemy, yelling as you do so. If you were from the Scottish Highlands in the sixteenth century, what you yelled might be a *sloggorne* – a word that has been spelled in various ways and sometimes even (by later and rather fanciful poets) *slughorn*, as if it were a sort of trumpet. It comes from the Gaelic for a war cry and was intended both to intimidate the enemy and to identify you to your allies. It's this second meaning that has survived since the moment when, in the nineteenth century, we turned the word into *slogan*, a distinctive phrase used in political rallies or in advertising, to make sure that anyone who hears it knows why they should vote for you or buy your recommended brand of toothpaste or cat food.

Other fighters who went wild and uttered bloodcurdling cries were the Old Norse warriors called the Berserkers. The name may mean either 'bare shirt' or 'bear shirt': no one is entirely sure, because it is known that in Ancient Roman times some tribes fought bare-chested while others wore bearskin hoods. (There were also some who wore wolfskin hoods, but they needn't distract us here.) However they may have dressed, the Berserkers fought, according to the OED, *in a frenzied fury known as the 'berserker rage'*. Their reputation lived on for almost two millennia, because as late as 1851 the novelist Charles Kingsley was describing someone as *Yelling, like Berserk fiends*, and still using the capital letter that indicated a proper name. The evolution of the term continued from there, so that in 1940 the *Chicago Tribune* could write disapprovingly of *The recent addition of the word 'berserk', as a synonym for crackpot behaviour, to the slang of the young and untutored*. Nowadays it's almost always heard as **to go berserk**, to lose your temper in a particularly frantic way: *My parents went berserk when I told them I didn't want to go to college – I've never seen them so angry.*

You could also describe what the Berserkers did as **running amok**, but this is a much later term and comes from Malay. This definition from a Malay dictionary published in 1812 was written by a man called William Marsden, who had served with the East India Company in Sumatra:

> *engaging furiously in battle, attacking with desperate resolution, rushing in a state of frenzy to the commission of indiscriminate murder.*

Today, **to run amok** (or the more English-looking **amuck**) is perhaps more physical than **to go berserk**: there are a number of twentieth-century quotations showing someone **running amok** with a chainsaw or other violent weapon, but schoolchildren can also **run amok** in the playground and dogs can do it in a park when they're let off the lead. You don't have to commit murder, only mayhem. (**Mayhem**, by the way, used also to imply physical injury: it's related to **maim**, but nowadays just means noisy chaos.)

In a calmer military arena…

…a medieval knight going into battle or into a jousting match would often tie a bunch of ribbons to his arms, or carry a glove or a handkerchief that had been given to him by a lady as a sign of her approval or *favour*. Such emblems were also called *favours* – the precursors of today's *party favours* or *wedding favours* – and were intended to be prominently displayed, so that everyone would know that the knight was committing acts of valour on behalf of the lady concerned. This may well be the origin of the concept of **wearing your heart on your sleeve**, making it clear what your feelings are or where your affections lie.

Such a knight, using French as the language of chivalry, would be mounted on **un grand cheval**, a great or **high horse**, from which we get **to be on your high horse,** to behave in a disdainful, self-righteous way, and related idioms such as **to get/come down off your high horse**, to stop being so conceited: *Oh, get off your high horse! It won't hurt you to help with the housework just this* *once*. These idiomatic uses date from the nineteenth century, when the age of chivalry – or at least of jousting – was very much a thing of the past.

A knight would normally owe allegiance to one lord or king, from Arthur back in the mists of legend to Henry VIII in the sixteenth century. His weapons, including the long spear-like device called a **lance**, would be at his master's service. Someone who was less loyal would offer himself to anyone who would pay him: he was described as having or being a **free lance** – **free** in the sense of not being tied to any one person or cause. By the nineteenth century the term was being applied to politicians who belonged to no particular party, and subsequently to journalists who hired themselves out to whoever had work available. It wasn't until the mid-twentieth century that the concept became sufficiently widespread among musicians, models and others to lose any obvious connection to its military origins and be written as a single word, **freelance**.

Knights did most of their fighting on horseback, but if you wanted to **steal a march** on someone, you had to be on foot. In the days of foot soldiers, a **march** was the distance covered during a certain period, usually a day, so if you **gained** or **stole a march**, you marched on when you might be expected to be resting, getting further ahead than the enemy expected.

Today, **to steal a march** is still to gain a surprise advantage over someone, but it can be found in many contexts that don't require you to stay up all night: *He stole a march on the other bidders by putting in a pre-emptive offer the day before the auction.*

In the days before guns...

...you might find yourself besieging a castle and wanting to blast a hole in the walls or blow the gate open. In these circumstances a **petard** would come in handy. It was a small bomb – the name comes from the French for a fart, so really *quite* a small bomb. But, just as you're warned against going back to a firework after you've lit it, you had to be careful to keep a distance from a lighted petard; otherwise it might explode and send you flying into the air, so that you were **hoist with your own petard**. The first figurative use of this – meaning to have your plans backfire on you, to be caught in a plot of your own making – comes in *Hamlet*, when the prince is being packed off to England with the untrustworthy Rosencrantz and Guildenstern. They have orders to kill him, but Hamlet plans to rearrange things so that it is Rosencrantz and Guildenstern who die:

> *Let it work,*
> *For 'tis the sport to have the engineer*
> *Hoist with his own petard.*

It was obviously Shakespeare rather than military history that popularized the expression: both Walter Scott and Thomas de Quincey, writing some two hundred years later, use it and acknowledge *Hamlet* as the source.

While the petards are exploding gently around your castle, you might be driven further and further inside it – surrendering control of the outer courtyard, retreating across the moat, behind one wall and then another as the enemy advances and you finally find yourself in ***the last ditch***, the last line of defence, a situation from which you are unlikely to recover. *A **last-ditch attempt***, then, is a final, desperate one, made after all other options have failed: *In a last-ditch attempt to break the deadlock, the delegates agreed to continue negotiations over the weekend.*

You'd think that a ***pikestaff*** might be something you carried into battle at about the same time as you were letting off petards, and indeed it was – the ***shaft*** of a ***pike***, a medieval spear. But a pikestaff was also a tall walking stick with a point or ***pike*** at the lower end, allowing you to stick it into the ground. There was also a ***packstaff***, on which an itinerant pedlar might rest his ***pack***. Brewer suggests that it was originally packstaffs that were plain, because the rubbing of the pack would have worn away any decoration it had – and a pedlar's staff wasn't likely to be highly decorated in the first place. The expression ***as plain as*** either ***a packstaff*** or ***a pikestaff*** existed by the sixteenth century, with alliteration obviously playing a part (as it did in establishing idioms such as **as right as rain**, **as fit as a fiddle**, **bats in the belfry** and many others). Early uses describe things that are plain in the sense of being undecorated; by the eighteenth century the more usual modern sense of obvious, needing no explanation, had taken over: *It's as plain as a pikestaff that he's lying through his teeth.*

In military circles from the sixteenth to the nineteenth centuries, **a forlorn hope** was a select body of men sent on ahead to begin an attack. You can see why this might have been **forlorn**, which originally meant lost or abandoned, but the **hope** part is more mysterious. It is, in fact, nothing to do with **hope** in the modern sense, but comes from a Dutch word that would more accurately be translated as **heap**. Confusion between the two has led to the contemporary meaning of a hope that has little chance of being fulfilled: *I'd love to be able to come with you, but it's a forlorn hope: I'm almost certainly working that weekend.*

In its modern sense **running the gauntlet** is an ordeal – it means exposing yourself to harsh treatment or criticism, from political opponents, the media or whoever – but it's nothing like as tough as it was in Sweden in the seventeenth century. Back then, it was a form of military discipline in which the person being punished was stripped to the waist and forced to run between two lines of men who beat him with sticks or knotted rope. The Swedish word was *gatlopp*, but it became confused with the French-derived *gauntlets*, heavy armoured gloves worn in medieval battles. A knight might *throw* or *fling* or *cast down the gauntlet* to issue a challenge to an opponent to engage in a jousting match or a duel; *picking up the gauntlet* signified acceptance of the challenge. Nowadays there are no gloves or knotted ropes involved: agreeing to eat the disgusting food offered to contestants on *I'm a Celebrity...Get Me Out of Here!* could be regarded as *picking up the gauntlet* – though come to think of it you might not want to handle fish eyes or pigs' testicles without wearing heavy gloves.

Someone wearing gauntlets might also be armed with *a double-edged sword*. Swords come in various types: the thrusting kind, like a rapier, intended to inflict a single, piercing blow; single-edged, like a scimitar, where only one edge of the blade is sharp; and double-edged, like a sabre, designed to enable you to slash it about in the heat of battle and not bother which way the blade is facing. You can inflict a lot of damage with a double-edged sword; the downside is that you can very easily hurt yourself as well. In modern terms, you might say that the growth of the search engine was *a double-edged sword*: it enables you to find answers quickly, but doesn't guarantee their accuracy. This also – and again by analogy with a sabre – *cuts both ways*.

In swordplay, a cut delivered across the body (from left to right if you're right-handed) is described as **back-handed,** just as a similar stroke in tennis is a **backhand**. In tennis there's nothing wrong with this – it's a necessary technique. But in fencing it's not the most straightforward approach, perhaps even a little sneaky. By 1800, therefore, the word had come to mean indirect, deceptive, so that a **back-handed compliment** is a form of verbal equivocation: is it a compliment or isn't it? It can be difficult to tell.

When guns came along...

Firearms began to replace swords in battle from about the fifteenth century. From the seventeenth to the nineteenth, a flintlock was a common way of making a gun fire. Pulling the trigger caused a flint to strike a piece of metal, producing a spark. This in turn ignited the gunpowder, which was stored in a compartment known as a **pan**. If the flint sparked but the gunpowder didn't ignite – perhaps because it was damp – the result was **a flash in the pan**, a brief burst of light that achieved little or nothing. The metaphorical use of this expression dates from the early nineteenth century, when this style of gun was still very much in use. It's found forty years before the California Gold Rush, which means that the alternative explanation (that prospectors were briefly excited when they saw a **flash** of light that looked like gold in the **pan** they used to wash earth from the metal) can't be true. A miner's pan is, however, responsible for **to pan out**: a *Manual of Mineralogy* of the period explained that *Gravel or soil…is said to* pan well *or* pan poorly *according to the result*. Today **panning out** may involve something as ordinary as how to get home at the end of an evening: *We could get the bus or find a taxi, depending on how things pan out.*

As gold is one of the most precious of metals, knowing whether you have the real thing or a brassy imitation can be important. One way of checking is to apply acid: unlike many other metals, gold does not react to nitric acid, but it does react to a mixture of nitric and hydrochloric. **An acid test**, then, will confirm whether or not what you are dealing with is gold; figuratively speaking, it is a rigorous and conclusive test of something's value: *Exam results are important, but the interview is the acid test of an applicant's calibre.*

Iron may not be precious but it is one of the strongest and hardest of metals and has been widely used in construction since the eighteenth century. Among the earliest things to be described as **ironclad** were warships, protected against attack by thick metal plates; nowadays something **ironclad** might be useful in a court of law: *He has an ironclad alibi for the night in question: he was giving a speech to over a thousand people.*

Going back to flintlocks, if yours was slow to ignite and didn't shoot as quickly as you expected, it was said to *hang fire* – hence the idea of putting off a decision: *Let's hang fire on opening another branch until we see how the first one does.*

Before you pull a trigger on certain types of gun you have to *cock* it – to draw back or raise part of the firing mechanism. If you raise it only halfway it is said to be *at half-cock*, so if something *goes off at half-cock* it goes off prematurely, before you are ready, and fails to achieve its aim: *The protest went off at half-cock because no one had thought to publicize the route of the march.*

A different sort of cock…

…gave rise to one military-sounding expression that has nothing to do with warfare. *A battle royal* comes from the barbaric but once extremely popular sport of cock-fighting, in which normally one bird or pair of birds was matched against another. *A battle royal* – whose name derives from the assumption that anything royal was magnificent and on a large scale – pitted all the competitors against each other at the same time, so that they fought it out until only one remained alive. The metaphorical idea of several people with strong opinions battling among themselves dates back as far as the seventeenth century, when the poet John Dryden applied it to various religious leaders who didn't see eye to eye. The concept of 'last man standing' has been diluted over the years: in twenty-first-century Britain you could equally find a battle royal between, say, Brexiteers and Remainers: only two factions, but a lot of conflict and damage. Despite the French influence on all sorts of early fighting vocabulary, *battle royal* seems always to have been spelled in this English way: it wasn't until the Japanese novel of 1999 that spawned two action films and a manga series that the more French-looking *Battle Royale* gained prominence.

Also drawn from cock-fighting is the image that links white feathers to cowardice. A thoroughbred fighting cock had no white on him, so a bird that *showed a white feather* wasn't likely to put up a good fight. It's because of this that, during World War One, women handed out white feathers in the street to apparently able-bodied men who weren't in uniform, accusing them of being too scared to join up.

The place where cocks fought was known as a *cockpit*: it was a sunken area (a *pit*) with seats rising in rows above it. From the sixteenth century on, *cockpit* came to denote other scenes of conflict: *the cockpit of Europe* often meant Belgium, which seemed to find itself at the centre of almost every European war (think Spanish Netherlands or Flanders Fields, depending on where your history specialism lies). Then the word moved into wider use: by the eighteenth century, the *cockpit* of a small boat was the sunken area where the helm was. At the beginning of the twentieth century, when racing cars and aeroplanes came along, a cockpit no longer needed to be lower than the main body of the vessel – the defining factor was now that it was the place where the controls were and where the driver or pilot sat.

Can't we be friends?

If you take an action that is likely to result in promotion if it succeeds or in demotion if it doesn't, you could be described as *chancing your arm* – in other words, running the risk of losing the stripes or other indications of rank that you wear on your sleeve. The idea of losing stripes is only one of two possible explanations, though. The other is endorsed by the website of St Patrick's Cathedral in Dublin, where, according to tradition, the leaders of two opposing clans clashed in the fifteenth century. Escaping from fierce fighting, the Butlers of Ormonde took refuge in the cathedral's chapter house, where their rivals, the FitzGeralds of Kildare, followed and demanded they come out and make peace. The Butlers, understandably, refused, whereupon the leader of the FitzGeralds ordered that a hole be cut in the door. He then thrust his arm through it in order to shake hands with his rival. Well, if he's willing to *chance his arm*, the Butlers decided, he must be sincere. A deal was done and the Door of Reconciliation, complete with hole, can still be seen in the cathedral.

In another form of reconciliation, across the Atlantic a couple of centuries later, the indigenous peoples used to **bury their hatchets** in the ground as a sign of peace. One European's seventeenth-century record of such a gesture remarked that this ceremony was, to the chiefs involved, *more significant & binding than all Articles of Peace, the Hatchet being a principal weapon with them*. To this day, ending an argument and letting bygones be bygones can be described as **burying the hatchet**.

Once the hatchet was buried, colonists and Native Americans might sit down to a **powwow** – a conference or just a friendly exchange of views, from an Algonquian word for a shaman or medicine man, who would presumably have been consulted if anything important were being discussed. Then, once the talking was over, a unit might **get its marching orders**. In the eighteenth century, this simply meant orders as to when and where it was to march, but it soon extended to the current meaning, of being sent away, usually in disgrace: *He was obviously going to ruin the party so I gave him his marching orders – I didn't want him in my house.*

Even more shameful was to be **drummed out** of your regiment – in the early eighteenth century a drum would be beaten in a certain rhythm as the disgraced soldier made his departure. Within a matter of decades this idea had caught on in civilian life, so that you can now be ***drummed out of town*** or ***drummed out of the bridge club*** without the accompaniment of a percussion instrument. Beating a drum can be a dull, repetitive action – though there are plenty of jazz musicians who prove that it doesn't have to be. It's that idea that allows you to ***drum*** information into someone's head or to ***drum up*** support for a cause by going around canvassing or repeating a sales pitch over and over again.

During the American Civil War in the 1860s, a line was drawn around a military prison; anyone who crossed that *line* while trying to escape was liable to be shot – possibly ***dead***. Thus ***a deadline*** became something that you crossed at your peril; by the 1920s it meant a date by which journalists had to deliver their copy, students hand in their assignments and so on. We now talk about ***missing*** rather than ***crossing*** a deadline and it isn't usually fatal, but it still has its drawbacks if you have an inflexible editor or tutor.

It was also the American Civil War that produced a Unionist hymn whose chorus went:

> *Hold the fort for we are coming.*
> *Union men, be strong!*
> *Side by side we battle onward;*
> *Victory will come.*

The composer and hymn writer Philip Bliss produced this verse after hearing a story – possibly apocryphal – that General William Sherman had sent a message saying, 'Hold the fort. I am coming' to a fellow general who was struggling to withstand a Confederate attack. The expression was in non-military use by the early twentieth century and now simply means to cope while someone else is absent: *Can you hold the fort if I nip out for a few minutes?*

Fast-forwarding to World War Two, posters warning that Careless Talk Costs Lives included a number of images that assumed the man of the house was the family breadwinner. The punning advice **Be Like Dad, Keep Mum** owed its origins to various forms of entertainment that had been popular several hundred years earlier. An old word **mum**, in use from the fifteenth century, meant to make a small and inarticulate sound; it was probably related to **mumble** and represented the sound it described: **mmmm**. There was also, in the sixteenth century, a dice game called **mumchance**. Traditionally played during carnival time, it became associated with wearing masks and hence with masquerades or dumb shows, sometimes known as **mumming** or **mummery**. These elements seem to have come together so that **to play mumchance** and **to keep mum** meant to keep silent, to refuse to speak. By the end of the sixteenth century, **mum** had also emerged as a casual word for **mother**, developing from the baby-talk **mama**. Having these two completely different meanings for **mum** was very convenient when the Ministry of Information came to design its posters in 1940.

World War Two also gave us the **blockbuster**: a bomb that could wipe out – or **bust** – an entire city **block**. After the war this devastating term quickly developed into a compliment: **a blockbuster of an idea** was a particularly clever and innovative one. Then Hollywood got hold of the word and applied it to massively expensive films such as the 1959 version of *Ben-Hur*, which cost over $15 million, the biggest budget ever at the time. From there a blockbuster also became the sort of lengthy novel you buy to read on holiday, often a sprawling family saga. The term has been widely adopted for commercial purposes: it's the name of various comic supervillains (presumably with reference to the destructive power of the original blockbusting bomb), several television game shows (with punning reference to the use of building blocks), a now defunct chain of movie rental stores, a board game about movies and much more, drifting further and further from the original meaning.

In more modern warfare, **ground zero** is the point on the ground directly under the explosion of a nuclear weapon in the air. It dates from 1946, when it was used in a report on the atomic bombs that American forces had dropped the previous year on the Japanese cities of Hiroshima and Nagasaki. After the 9/11 attacks in 2001, Ground Zero came to refer specifically to the area around the devastated Twin Towers of the World Trade Center in New York; it also now refers casually to any completely new beginning, one that involves A CLEAN SLATE (see page 76).

Zero hour, the moment when a military operation is due to begin, is earlier, dating from World War One. By the 1920s it had achieved wider circulation and can now be used for the start of any significant event: *It's almost zero hour – the match kicks off in ten minutes.*

Which sounds like a good excuse to turn the page and go on to the chapter about sport.

CHAPTER 6

Currying Favour with No Holds Barred

The origins of many sports and games go back hundreds of years, although the rules may have changed considerably over time. We Anglophones have obviously taken these leisure activities seriously, as a surprising amount of their vocabulary has spilled over into more general use. Let's **set the ball rolling** and see what happens.

Brewer's *Dictionary of Phrase and Fable* defines **to keep the ball rolling** as 'to continue without intermission. To keep the fun, conversation, or the matter going.' It goes on to explain, not very helpfully, that it is 'a metaphor from ball games'. The same goes for **to set/start the ball rolling**, meaning to initiate an idea or a conversation: *We hope everyone will contribute to the discussion, but would someone like to set the ball rolling? It's* not obvious which game was the inspiration – bowls, perhaps, in which it is useful for the bowl to keep rolling towards the jack? The expression has been around only since the eighteenth century, by which time some form of bowls had been known in England for five hundred years, giving plenty of opportunity for a metaphor to develop.

We can be slightly clearer about *the ball is in your court* – it's your turn, it's up to you to take action. This isn't recorded before the mid-twentieth century and is a development of the earlier *the ball is with you*. So either you are in control of the situation (because you're in possession of the ball) or you ought to get rid of it as quickly as possible and make things happen. This obviously comes from a game that involves a court, most likely tennis, but has always had wider uses: *I've sent him an invitation, but now the ball is in his court – it's up to him whether he comes or not.*

Real tennis, a game that was popular in Tudor times (*real* in this context means 'royal' and you can still see where Henry VIII played it at Hampton Court), is played indoors; it's the precursor of modern tennis but in many ways is more like squash. The net is tied to a post at one side of the court; a pillar supports the spectators' stands at the other side. Knocking the ball *from pillar to post*, therefore, makes your opponent run around a great deal and achieve very little. By the time the expression first appeared in print, in 1500 and in its original form of *from post to pillar*, it was being used in a metaphorical sense. That was in the anonymous allegorical poem *The Assembly of the Gods*, in which the central character, in order to appease the gods he sees in a dream, goes through a form of penance that drives him from Contrition to Satisfaction, *thus from post to pillar he was made to dance*. It's also suggested that the expression was switched to its current form (as early as 1550) because a poet wanted to use it and *post* was easier to rhyme than *pillar*. The modern version was well established by the late nineteenth century: in Thomas Hardy's *Tess of the d'Urbervilles*, published in 1891, Tess's father, a humble pedlar, on hearing that he may be descended from a noble family, exclaims:

> *And here have I been knocking about, year after*
> *year, from pillar to post, as if I was no more than*
> *the commonest feller in the parish…*

He means that, instead of being a gentleman of leisure, as befits his ancestry, he's been doing odd jobs, struggling to make ends meet, just like that real tennis player who was running all over the court.

It's possible that *love* meaning 'no score' in tennis (found since the eighteenth century) comes from the vaguely similar-sounding French *l'oeuf*, meaning 'the egg', because an elongated figure zero could be seen as resembling an egg. That's certainly where we get the expression *out for a duck* (out without scoring) in cricket – it's short for **duck's egg** and has been used in that abbreviated form since the 1860s.

Cricket and baseball

A **hat trick**, which can now apply to a footballer scoring three goals in the same match, a competitor in any sport winning three consecutive Olympic gold medals and various other three-in-a-row successes, is also originally a cricketing term. In the nineteenth century, so legend has it, a bowler who took three wickets with three successive balls either won a hat or had a hat passed round the ground to collect donations and was entitled to take the proceeds. But why a trick, rather than a wicket? Well, we're in 'best guess' territory here but it may be because it seemed like a conjuring trick. A hat trick is a rare event – there have been just forty-four of them in over a hundred and forty years of test cricket – so perhaps achieving this feat was likened to a magician pulling a rabbit out of a hat.

A bowler capable of taking a hat trick isn't often **hit for six**, but it does happen. Batters score six runs if they hit the ball over the boundary without it bouncing – it's the highest score generally available off a single ball. Bowlers who are **hit for six**, then, suffer the worst fate possible. So, since the 1930s, does anyone who is idiomatically **hit** or **knocked for six**: they are completely overcome or humiliated. A plan or project can suffer the same fate: *Our plans for moving to the country were knocked for six when the survey found dry rot in the house we wanted to buy.*

Being hit for six, on or off the cricket field, may be a sign that you've lost control of the situation. But you can regain it by doing something *off your own bat*. In cricket, there are various ways of scoring, but runs are credited to your name only if you hit the ball with the bat (or if it comes off your gloves, but this isn't the place to delve into the niceties of cricket). So something you do *off your own bat* uses your initiative and your own efforts: *The surveyor didn't seem to be doing anything, so we called in a dry-rot expert off our own bat.* Interestingly, the OED's earliest citation is dated 1742, twenty years before the foundation of the Hambledon Club that is traditionally considered the 'home of cricket'; it also refers to someone getting *forty notches off his own bat*. You don't scores notches in modern cricket, so the idiom must date back to an earlier form of the game.

In addition to there being various ways of scoring, there are no fewer than ten ways to be out. One of them is to be *stumped*, and it might be tempting to assume that this was the origin of being stumped in the sense of being confused or at a loss. Not so: as long ago as 1250 *to stump* meant to stumble over a tree stump or similar obstacle, and in the early nineteenth century American settlers were frequently *stumped* when their plough hit something solid that hadn't been cleared from the land they were trying to cultivate.

So much for cricket. It's from baseball that we get the image of an idea or suggestion *coming out of left field*, meaning coming out of the blue and being slightly bizarre, not following logically from what was being discussed before. It's the nature of baseball that outfielders are not as closely involved with every ball as the players positioned nearer to the batting plate, so the idea that they could mentally drift off for a moment is reasonable enough. But that the person in the left field position should be more distracted than the one on the right or in the centre is illogical: right-handed batters tend to pull the ball to their left, so the left fielder should be the busiest of the three. One not very satisfactory explanation relies on the fact that Babe Ruth, perhaps the greatest baseball player of all time, was left-handed, so would have hit the ball to the right and allowed the left fielder more leisure. A more likely suggestion is that the idiom comes from the deep-rooted idea that anything from the left (which in Latin is *sinister* and in French is *gauche*, so you may notice a trend) is bound to be unconventional.

From baseball, too, comes *a rain check*. One of the many meanings of *check* is a ticket or other receipt used to identify property deposited somewhere like a left-luggage office (*baggage check*) or a cloakroom (*hat check*). In the USA in the 1880s, a baseball manager called Abner Powell came up with the bright idea of issuing tickets with a detachable stub (or *check*), so that if a match was rained off you could exchange your check for a ticket admitting you to a later game. The idea soon spread to other arenas – in 1917 one enterprising theatre owner was offering a rain check to anyone suffering from bronchitis, encouraging them to stay away if they were likely to cough their way through a performance. From here, *to take a rain check* developed into a way of turning down an invitation with the promise of accepting it later: *I'd love to come to dinner, but I have an early start the next day – may I take a rain check?*

A hundred years and more ago, baseball was sometimes known as *hardball*, for the simple reason that it was played with a harder ball than *softball*. Softball tended to be played by children and women, with the implication that hardball was for serious athletes and tough guys. Hence the idiom that emerged in the 1970s: *playing hardball* in the business sense means using tough, uncompromising tactics in order to achieve your ends, the sort of thing that might then have been seen as a strictly masculine activity. Not any more, though; you could easily say *Mum* (or perhaps *Mom*, as it's still quite an American expression) *always plays hardball at bedtime – she insists our lights are out by eight o'clock.*

A good walk spoiled

Then there's golf, with its odd scoring system of *birdies* and *bogies* and *eagles*. If you don't do anything brilliant or disastrous you end up with *par*: the number of strokes that a good player is likely to take on a particular hole or course. Although golf in some form or another has been played in Scotland since the fifteenth century, the rules weren't standardized until the late nineteenth, which is when the concept of *par* became widespread; by the middle of the twentieth century the metaphorical *par for the course*, meaning what was to be expected, was established too. There's often a feeling of disappointment about it: *I waited half an hour for a bus, which is par for the course on a Saturday afternoon.*

The bird-related terms aren't generally used away from the golf course, but there's a nice story attached to them. A *birdie* – completing a hole with one stroke fewer than par – comes from the American slang use of *bird* to mean a person or thing that is in some way excellent. Tradition has it that a golfer called George Crump hit a fine second shot on a par-four hole at the Atlantic City County Club in 1903; the ball landed close to the hole and Crump, remarking that that had been *a bird of a shot*, agreed with his two companions that he would win double the usual money if he 'holed out' with his next stroke, scoring one under par. (This, for the benefit of non-golfers, is a good thing: in golf, the fewer strokes you take, and therefore the lower your score, the better.) He duly did and the three players thereafter referred to such a stroke as a *birdie*. A plaque at the hole commemorates the event to this day.

Within a very few years of this incident, going one better than Crump had done – completing a hole in two under par – became known as an *eagle*, an eagle being rather more impressive than any old bird. The rare achievement of going three under par is in the USA generally known as a *double eagle*, but elsewhere goes by the name of another spectacular bird, an *albatross*.

Bogey, bizarrely, is related to an old music-hall song about a *bogey-man* – a goblin or demon with a threatening presence. The song was popular in 1890 and it's said that a certain Major Wellman, playing at Great Yarmouth golf club in that year, came across the concept of par for the first time. According to this system, players are not so much competing against other golfers as pitting themselves against the course. Realizing that he was falling short of the ideal and thinking of the song, the major is said to have exclaimed, 'This player of yours [the imaginary one who set the standard for the course] is a regular bogey-man.' The term having caught on, it became a synonym of par for the next fifty years, before drifting to mean one over par, the widely accepted meaning today.

The fighting spirit

Early in the nineteenth century a boxer would literally *throw his hat into the ring* to indicate a willingness to fight and *throw in the towel* to concede defeat. Both expressions soon moved away from the sporting arena and into the wider world: *At last night's press conference she officially threw her hat into the ring, confirming that she would run for mayor in the next election* or *I've tried and tried but I just can't raise enough money: I guess it's time to throw in the towel.*

Before feeling obliged to throw in the towel, a boxer might be forced *on to the back foot* and/or *against the ropes*, both indicating that their opponent was in control, dictating how and where the struggling combatant could stand. (That dominant fighter might also be said *to have the upper hand* – to have an advantage or be in a position of power – but that expression was first used in military rather than sporting contexts.) According to the Queensberry Rules, which in the 1860s standardized the rules of boxing under the auspices of the 9th Marquess of Queensberry, *to hit below the belt* is a foul. It's now also any discourteous and unkind action, as in *It was hitting below the belt to mention how wild he'd been as a teenager, given that he's turned forty now and hasn't been in trouble for years.*

Queensberry's interest was in boxing, but wrestling was also regulated towards the end of the nineteenth century. Different styles of wrestling permit or forbid different holds, so the roughest, toughest form is the one with *no holds barred* – in other words, anything goes, whether above or below the belt. Away from wrestling, something done with *no holds barred* could be verbal or legal rather than physical: *Once they had finally decided to divorce they fought with no holds barred.*

It isn't only in boxing that you could **beat the living daylights out of someone** – indeed, the Marquess of Queensberry would probably have ruled that the fight should be stopped before that happened. **Daylights** was eighteenth- and nineteenth-century slang for the eyes, so **to darken someone's daylights** was to give them a black eye or two and to **beat the daylights** out of them was to beat them so hard that their eyes fell out, though it's to be hoped that this wasn't often taken literally. There are now a number of variations on this theme: a powerful horror film might **scare the living daylights out of you**; a particularly violent person might **beat the living hell out of you**, and so on. **Living** in this context has no real connection to life or death, it's just a vague intensifier, as in *He's the living spit of his father*, meaning he's very like him indeed.

If you chose, for whatever reason, not to fight as hard as you could, you might **pull your punches**, meaning that you let them fall short of the target or land more gently than they might have done. This expression, first recorded in the 1930s, seems always to have been used in a figurative sense, meaning to be gentle or tolerant in expressing an opinion, and is often used negatively: *The review pulled no punches – the critic made it clear that she thought the play was rubbish.*

The idea of matching two fighters of approximately equal weight dates back to well before Queensberry, but the current classifications were established in the early twentieth century. Obviously a disparity of weight favoured the heavier boxer, but a particularly skilful or feisty lightweight might **punch above his weight**. By the 1980s, that idea was being applied outside the boxing ring, perhaps to a small company that achieved surprisingly good results against stiff competition from the **heavyweights** in its field: *Several of the smaller funds punched above their weight in terms of return on investment, achieving results the gilt-edged securities couldn't better.*

A bow at a venture

Another sport that has been around for a long time is archery, where **having more than one string to your bow** means having something to fall back on if the first attempt fails: *Finishing her degree in chemistry gave her another string to her bow in case she didn't make it as a singer.* The shorter, thicker kind of arrow used in a crossbow (a weapon that's been known in Europe since Ancient Greek times, about two and a half thousand years) is sometimes known as a **bolt**. You can't reload a crossbow and fire quickly again and again, the way a skilled archer can with a long bow. So if you **have shot your bolt**, you have used up all your ammunition, done all you can, a metaphor that can be found in texts dating back as far as the twelfth century.

Horse and hound

In sporting terms, horse racing is one of the richest source of idioms. *To win hands down* – to win easily and resoundingly – was originally something a jockey did if he was well ahead of the field at the end of a race: it meant he didn't have to raise his *whip hand*, nor keep his hands tight on the reins by the horse's neck. The idea of *having the whip hand over someone* has been around since the seventeenth century, nearly a hundred years before the Jockey Club established the rules of horse racing. But anyone driving a horse and cart (or indeed a horse and chariot in Roman times) would have carried a whip to help them control and encourage their animals; the same is true of slave owners and Dickensian schoolmasters. The metaphor doesn't imply violence or even necessarily unfairness, but it does mean you have an advantage over someone: *Having been with the company so long gave him a whip hand over the newcomers who didn't understand the system.*

The opposite of being won hands down, a race or anything else that goes *down to the wire* isn't decided until the very last minute. The image comes from the days before photographs were taken on the course, when a wire was strung across the track above the finishing line to help the stewards decide the result of a close-run race. This would have been particularly useful if the leaders were running *neck and neck* – an expression that had moved off the racecourse and been extended to people in a close-run political contest by the early nineteenth century.

The original **dark horses** weren't necessarily dark at all; they had merely been **kept dark**, or the public had been **kept in the dark** about their form and prospects. **A dark horse**, in other words and from about the 1830s, came from nowhere and won unexpectedly. Only a few years later, the description was applied to James K. Polk, who surprised everyone by beating two-times previous candidate Senator Henry Clay to become eleventh President of the United States in 1845. Since then **a dark horse** can be anyone who has a surprising success or, in the run-up to any kind of contest, is little known but shouldn't be written off: *Tanya is favourite to win the 200 metres, but you might like to keep an eye on Chris – she's a dark horse.*

Perhaps surprisingly, **currying favour** – ingratiating yourself with your boss or with members of a club you are eager to join – is also connected with horses and has nothing to do with spicy cookery. It refers to the sort of **currying** you do with a **curry comb** – basically grooming a horse. **Favour** in this context doesn't mean favour as we understand it; it harks back to a medieval French story about a horse called **Fauvel** who became so important that he lived in a palace rather than a stable and even the nobility went to grovel to him. They would do anything they could to earn his approval, including grooming or currying him, a lowly task normally left to a servant. **Currying**

Fauvel is another of those expressions (see MUMBO-JUMBO, page 138) that has changed over the years as people have lost sight of its origins, thought, 'That can't be right' and adapted it to something more familiar.

In the hunting world, 'Hark, hounds, back' was a call to foxhounds that had run ahead of the scent, instructing them to come back until they picked up the trail again. Thus *to hark back* was to retrace one's steps and now particularly refers to being reminiscent of something earlier: *The guitarist's style harked back to the glory days of the Rolling Stones.*

It's often suggested that *drawing a red herring* across the hounds' path was a way of distracting them from the chase – a red herring being a smoked and therefore powerfully scented one. But this seems unlikely: as the Phrase Finder website remarks, there was no hunt saboteur movement in the seventeenth century, when this practice is first described. Perhaps, the site continues, getting the hounds to follow a red herring was a training exercise, before they were let loose on a live fox. Phrase Finder also recounts the tale of a wealthy seventeenth-century clergyman who left to his servant 'something that would make him drink' after his master's death. The servant was understandably disappointed when the bequest turned out to be a salted herring, which would certainly make him thirsty when he ate it but wasn't exactly what he had been hoping for. It's not clear which of these explanations, if any, gave rise to the figurative ***red herrings*** – distractions and irrelevancies – found in various non-hunting contexts. In the early nineteenth century the expression usually referred to politicians trying to distract attention from the real issues; by the twentieth it had become popular with writers of detective fiction who wanted to throw their readers off the scent. In 1931 Dorothy L. Sayers published a detective novel called *The Five Red Herrings*, set in a fishing village and featuring six suspects (of whom five are, of course, there to distract the reader from the real culprit); in 1994 Jeffrey Archer went several steps further with a collection of short stories entitled *Twelve Red Herrings*, in which the reader is challenged to find the misleading strand in each of the twelve tales.

Back on the hunting field, another of the hounds' tasks was to find a fox that had taken refuge in its lair or ***earth***, which wasn't always an easy thing to do. By the middle of the nineteenth century ***to run someone to earth*** had come to mean to find them after an exhaustive search: *I looked everywhere for him and finally ran him to earth in the garden shed.*

Poaching has always been a problem in the hunting world. From the eleventh century laws were passed to control who killed what where. Anything you were permitted to take was ***fair game***, an idea that now has a broad remit: *Fashions in satire have changed over the years, but politicians will always be fair game.*

It was obviously important to protect the areas that housed game – often deer, in royal hunting grounds. But some concessions had to be made to peasants needing to sustain themselves. They were allowed to go onto what was called common land, which was deemed to belong to everyone in the parish or manor. There they might gather dead wood and other things that would serve as fuel or food. To do this they were entitled to use various sorts of *hooked* pole, including one like a shepherd's *crook*. Thus *by hook or by crook* came to signify by any means available, by fair means or foul. That's the most probable explanation, anyway, and the expression was well established by the sixteenth century. *Crook* meaning a criminal is much later – nineteenth-century USA – and simply implies that such a person's conduct is *crooked*, off the straight and narrow.

One final note on horses. The word *steeplechase* conjures up a wonderfully rural English image, and rightly so: it has always been a race or *chase* in which obstacles (fences, water, etc.) had to be cleared. As the name suggests its finishing point was originally – in the eighteenth century – the church *steeple*.

As good as a rest

Mention of steeples brings us to another quintessentially English occupation: bell-ringing. In this, a *change* is defined as any of the various orders in which a peal of bells can be rung, so a row of five bells might be rung in the order 1 2 3 4 5, followed by 2 1 4 3 5 (where each of the first four bells has changed places with its neighbour), followed by 2 4 1 5 3 (where the last four have changed places) and so on. Following a sequence such as this is known as *ringing the changes*, and indeed many serious campanologists would describe their sport as *change-ringing* rather than *bell-ringing*. In a non-bell-ringing context, therefore, *to ring the changes* is to change them in an orderly fashion, to go through the options. This line from the romantic novelist Georgette Heyer, writing in 1951, gives the true spirit: *The Dowager harangued him for half an hour, ringing all the changes between scolding, dictating, and pleading.* Since then, we've tended to use the expression more loosely, but, for example, being tired of pastel colours and *ringing the changes by painting the kitchen walls yellow and the cabinets orange* isn't strictly *ringing the changes*, it's just altering your colour scheme.

Cards on the table

We mentioned a score of *love* in tennis and a *duck* in cricket (see page 117), but there are terms for being soundly beaten or not scoring at all in card games as well. In North America, you can be *skunked* at various games, presumably because, in addition to being a smelly animal, a skunk is also a contemptible person. In more refined circles and specifically in the card games bezique and piquet, you might be *rubiconed*. This is a reference to Julius

Caesar crossing the River Rubicon in northern Italy in 49 BC: it was significant because he had an army at his back, which meant that the action broke Roman law and precipitated civil war. **Crossing the Rubicon** (still usually with an initial capital) has come to mean reaching a point of no return, committing yourself to an action from which there is no turning back. In the card games, the penalty for losing is greater if you fail to reach that critical point.

To digress for a moment from cards, another way of reaching a point of no return is **to burn your bridges** or **to burn your boats** behind you. This presupposes that you have just crossed a river and while on the one hand you are preventing your enemy from following you, on the other you are cutting off any chance of retreat. Both expressions are found in a non-military sense in the nineteenth century and can be applied to anything from politics to your private life: *The announcement really burned the minister's boats: the backbenchers were furious and she'll never get them to support her* or *Don't burn your bridges with your grandfather: he'll leave his money to charity if you upset him.* Bridges and boats can be used interchangeably here: they are equally impossible to rebuild once the damage has been done.

Anyway, back to losing at cards. Another way of describing the position at the end of a game is **the lurch**: the point at which a player wins not by achieving a specific score but by being a certain number of points ahead of their opponent. The losing player is therefore **left in the lurch**. It's an idea that has been around since the late sixteenth century and was almost immediately given the non-card-playing sense of being abandoned unexpectedly, without support or hope of rescue: *I'm sorry to leave you in the lurch but the car has broken down and I won't be able to pick you up.* This sort of **lurch** has nothing to do with the sudden movement of a ship in rough seas; it comes from the French **lourche**, a sixteenth-century game resembling backgammon. In backgammon, by the way, there are two levels of being badly beaten: a **gammon** and, even worse, a **backgammon**. **Gammon** in this context is related to the Old English for **game** rather than the cured pork of that name. The latter derives from an Old Northern French word **gambe**, the equivalent of the modern **jambe**, meaning leg.

In the USA in the nineteenth century, poker players used to place a small token in front of the player whose turn it was to bet. Once that player had placed his bet, the token was passed to the next player, and so on round the table. Why this token should have been called a **buck** is unclear; it's highly unlikely that a dollar bill was used and there's no convincing evidence that it was a piece of buckshot – it could equally well have been a pocket knife or the stub of a pencil. But this is the origin of *to pass the buck*, to shift responsibility to someone else, which had become a non-poker-related colloquialism by the early twentieth century: *We made the decision together, but now he's trying to pass the buck on to me by saying that it was all my idea.* When, in the 1940s, US President Harry S. Truman famously put a sign on his desk saying, 'The buck stops here', he meant that he had no one to *pass the buck* to: he had to take responsibility for anything that happened.

A group of poker players sitting round a kitchen table might bet with cash; in a casino or other more formal setting you are more likely to buy counters known as *chips* which have a designated value and can be 'cashed in' (if there are any left) at the end of the night. Once you've placed your chips into the pot at poker or on your chosen number at roulette, you've made your commitment and there's no going back – *the chips are down*. From here we get the idea of a moment of crisis, something that tests someone's mettle: *She may seem a bit scatty but when the chips are down you can depend on her.* (She may even, to use a metaphor from a different card game, *turn up trumps*.) If you *cash in your chips* or, more recently, *have had your chips* you have been beaten or even killed: *A lot of the pilots cashed in their chips in that raid* or *The business will never recover from those losses – I'm afraid he's had his chips.*

Continuing the gambling theme, the first official lottery in England dates back to the time of Queen Elizabeth I, although the concept probably existed before that and winning tickets were simply those that had a number printed on them. If you *drew a blank*, you lost. Since at least the early twentieth century, the expression has had a figurative use: *The committee tried to recruit more volunteers, but drew a complete blank.*

The sort of lottery in which all the participants buy a ticket which gives them, say, a horse in a forthcoming race, has followed an unusual evolutionary path. A *sweepstake* used to be someone or something who won or took everything – in Tudor times it was commonly used as the name of a boat, one that swept all before her, in a similar spirit to the later *dreadnought*, which *dreaded nought* or was afraid of nothing. It wasn't until the eighteenth century that *sweepstake* came to mean the prize to be won in a winner-takes-all competition and not until the nineteenth that it acquired its usual modern meaning of the competition or transaction itself: *We always have an office sweepstake during the World Cup.*

The dicing game of hazard, very popular in Regency England (the early nineteenth century), involved calling out the number you intended to throw before you cast the dice. Probably from the French for a hand, this was known as a *main*. *To have an eye for the main chance,* to care only about what might be best for yourself, is likely to be connected with this usage, though *main* in the sense of 'most important' comes into it too.

It's magic

Predicting what you are going to achieve may also be the origin of *to call the shots*: around the start of the twentieth century, marksmen giving an exhibition of shooting would announce which part of the target they intended to hit. By the middle of the century this had come to refer to a person who dictated actions or policies: *The President may be nominally in charge, but it's his Chief of Staff who calls the shots.*

When it came to predicting what was going to happen, the Ancient Romans were great ones for omens: they would examine the entrails of dead birds or the flight path of live ones in order to decide if a particular day was auspicious for, say, a journey or a marriage. In fact, this is where the word *auspicious* comes from: the priest who conducted these investigations was an *auspex* or *augur*, names connected with the Latin *avis*, meaning bird. So something that was *auspicious* passed the bird-examining test: the conditions were favourable and the event could go ahead. Today, you can do research *under the auspices* of a certain university (that is, with its support and approval) or join a club *under the auspices* of a friend who is already a member. There doesn't need to be a bird in sight.

Moving from one era's superstitions to another's, Thomas Ady's seventeenth-century treatise on witchcraft, *A Candle in the Dark*, mentions the conjurors who performed at fairs and markets. One of these apparently called himself *The Kings Majesties most excellent Hocus Pocus… because that at the playing of every Trick, he used to say,* Hocus pocus, tontus talontus, vade celeriter jubeo, *a dark composure of words, to blinde the eyes of the beholders, to make his Trick pass the more currantly without discovery, because when the eye and the ear of the beholder are both earnestly busied, the Trick is not so easily discovered.*

This fake Latin must have been in use long before Ady recorded it, because **hocus pocus** as a synonym for conjuror or juggler appears thirty years earlier. Then it became a general pseudo-magic word along the lines of **abracadabra** and **hanky-panky**: the latter nowadays usually refers to some form of sexual dalliance, but was coined in the nineteenth century to mean sleight of hand or trickery. By about that time **hocus pocus** had moved away from a magician's performance and come to mean a more general kind of deception – not so much **abracadabra** as GOBBLEDYGOOK (see page 39). Or indeed **mumbo-jumbo**, a word derived in the eighteenth century from the name of a West African god and adopted into English as a term for nonsense – often the sort of nonsense that is surrounded by ritual or high-flown language intended to impress. In 1870, Louisa Alcott, author of *Little Women*, conveyed the spirit of the term when she was travelling in France and wrote home to her mother: *We…went to vespers in the old church, where we saw a good deal of mumbo-jumbo by red, purple, and yellow priests.* There was a time when it looked as if **mumbo-jumbo** was going to be superseded by *mumble-jumble*, presumably because people who weren't well up on West African deities thought they must have got the word wrong and replaced it with something that made sense to them. Lots of English terms have evolved in the way they have for this reason (see, for example, APPLE-PIE ORDER on page 53 and CURRYING FAVOUR on page 128), but clearly the gods were on the side of *mumbo-jumbo* and it managed to hold its own.

All the fun of the fair

English is full of rhyming compound words. *Higgledy-piggledy* means in no particular order, in a confused heap. Its origins are uncertain, but it may be connected with pigs, which gather together in a chaotic way. It's been around since the sixteenth century. *Willy-nilly* is seventeenth century and comes from *will I, nill I* (or *will he, nill he*), where *will* means to wish or be willing and *nill* is the opposite. Thus *willy-nilly* was with good will or without it, whether I/you/they like it or not. Over the years it has drifted towards meaning something more like disorganized, haphazard, *higgledy-piggledy*. But there may still be a suggestion of unwillingness: *The children wanted to stay home and play with their iPads, but I bundled them into the car and took them to the park willy-nilly.*

Then there's *shilly-shally* (eighteenth century). This started life as *Shill I? Shall I?*, with its implication of dithering and being unable to make a decision: *Will you make up your mind? I don't want to stand here all day shilly-shallying.* Not to mention ***dilly-dally***, found first as a noun meaning hesitancy in the late sixteenth century and as a verb a hundred and fifty years later: it's a variation on the straightforward ***dally***, to spend time frivolously, to linger, famously recalled in the 1919 music-hall song:

> *My old man said, 'Follow the van*
> *And don't dilly-dally on the way.'*

The singer, unfortunately for her, ***dillied and dallied, dallied and dillied***, lost her way and didn't know where to roam. A warning to those inclined to loiter for no reason (and, in some versions of the song, nip into the pub).

The sixteenth century ***helter-skelter***, meaning in a carelessly hurried way, is another in the same vein. It may be what the OED calls an 'echoic' word, one that imitates the sound that it's describing, in this case hurrying feet. The ***helter-skelter*** down which you slide at a fairground takes its name from this style of movement and dates only from the early twentieth century, when the first ***helter-skelter lighthouse*** was built as part of the annual Hull Fair.

Another bit of fun at medieval fairs – in addition to conjurors spouting pseudo-Latin – was the game of ***fast and loose***. A gullible punter would spend good money to have a go at passing a stick through a loop in a rolled-up strap, unaware that the strap was not tied *fast* but that the showman could *loosen* it at a moment's notice. Shakespeare refers to the game in *Antony and Cleopatra*, but the broader idea of *playing fast and loose* with someone's affections or with one's responsibilities, of being inconstant and unreliable, was already familiar in the Bard's day. It crops up in his *King John*, in which one character (not the perfidious John, obviously) refuses to *play fast and loose with faith*, meaning that he won't break a promise he has made.

Since time immemorial, one of the things you've been able to do at a fairground is buy something *tawdry*. Chambers Dictionary defines this as *showy without taste or worth* – tat, in other words, and cheap-looking, gaudy tat at that. But why *tawdry*? Well, in the seventh century AD an East Anglian princess called Ethelthryth was Abbess of Ely. Under the name Etheldreda or Audrey she became an Anglo-Saxon saint (Ely Cathedral used to be dedicated to her) and a fair in her honour was held in Ely each October. Among the goods offered for sale were silk neckties or laces for women, which were a symbol of the saint. (*Lace* here means a decorative cord – think *necklace* or *shoelace* rather than the delicate fabric.) By the seventeenth century the quality of these laces had deteriorated to the extent that *St Audrey's lace* or, if you say it quickly, *tawdry lace* had become an epitome of tasteless flashiness. In due course the *lace* was dropped, so that you can now have *tawdry silver*

bracelets, *tawdry ornaments* or even *a tawdry excuse for a politician* if such a person has superficial charm but is tacky and untrustworthy underneath.

More fairground amusement came from using cards – particularly tarot cards – to tell people's fortunes. This became popular in the UK in the eighteenth century; if something was *on the cards* it was likely to happen. Charles Dickens' Mr Micawber (in *David Copperfield*), was trying everything he could to stay out of debtors' prison:

> *By way of going in for anything that might be on the cards, [he] composed a petition to the House of Commons, praying for an alteration in the law of imprisonment for debt.*

Looking to the future isn't the only superstition that has affected English vocabulary. We have over the centuries had some strange ideas about the human body, about colours associated with different aspects of it, and about colours themselves. Read on.

CHAPTER 7

Assassins, Thugs and Morticians

Medieval medicine, based on an Ancient Greek theory, believed that the human body contained four humours or fluids – blood, phlegm, black bile and yellow bile – and that an excess or deficiency of any one of them caused disease. Each humour was associated with a personality type: black bile was melancholic, blood was cheerful (or sanguine, from the French **sang,** meaning blood), and so on. We'll come back to the attributes of the various colours in a moment, but first, it wasn't just the 'humours' that were connected with emotions; most of the body's organs had their significance too.

An organ recital

The heart is the organ of courage as well as of love, so if **your heart is in your boots** you're terrified or miserable; if it's **in your mouth** you're nervous, waiting for something awful to happen. The idea that **your heart bleeds** for someone when you feel sorry for them can be traced back to the late fourteenth century, though the unpleasant **bleeding heart** as in **a bleeding-heart liberal**, someone the speaker thinks worries unnecessarily about social injustice, global warming or other such trivialities, dates only from the mid-twentieth and first appears in hard-boiled thrillers. Something that makes your heart bleed may also **tug at your heartstrings**, from another old (fifteenth century or earlier) idea that there were cord-like structures around the heart to support it.

Pouring your heart out – letting your emotions flow out of you, as if you were pouring them from a jug – goes back at least to the sixteenth century, while someone being **after your own heart** – in sympathy with your views and approach to life – is even older. It is found in Old English, as early as the eleventh century, and became widely used from the fifteenth, when it appeared in a translation of the Bible: in the first Book of Samuel, God, angry with King Saul, seeks a replacement and wants **a man after His own heart**. That man turns out to be David, an ancestor of Jesus and one of the most important figures of the Old Testament.

No wonder the God-fearing folk reading this expression in the fifteenth century took it *to their hearts*, as it were.

Courage, love and the pouring out of emotions aren't an end to the heart's perceived properties: it was also the seat of the intellect. *To know by heart* or *to learn by heart*, to know something from memory or to be able to repeat it without prompting, came into being by the fourteenth century. If the idea had emerged later we might be saying *I know it off by brain* – which, although logical enough, just doesn't sound right.

The liver, once believed to be the place where blood was produced, was also associated with courage: if you were *white-livered* or *lily-livered*, your liver didn't produce enough blood to make it a healthy colour – in other words, you were a coward. Or, in later American slang, a *yellow belly* – though that dates from a time when the expanding United States were at war with Mexico, so is probably an insulting allusion to the colour of the enemy's skin rather than a reference to his organs.

The kidneys seem to have had a broad remit: *a man of my kidney* means 'someone like me, a man of my nature or class'. Its first recorded use is in a ranting speech by the comical Sir John Falstaff in Shakespeare's *The Merry Wives of Windsor*, so it may initially have been intended as a joke. It went on to be used in a perfectly straight-faced way, however: if, in the nineteenth century, you described someone as *of the right kidney* you were giving them your SEAL OF APPROVAL (see page 64).

The stomach, too, was once seen as the seat of passion or emotion: Elizabeth I famously rallied her troops before their fight against the Spanish Armada in 1588 with a speech declaring, 'I know I have the body but of a weak and feeble woman; but I have the heart and stomach of a king, and of a king of England too.' To say that you **have the stomach** for something (or, more usually, that you haven't) means that you have (or haven't) the courage to do it, that you can (or can't) do it without feeling queasy. Less elegantly, you might **have the guts** to do something, which means the same thing.

To have someone's guts for garters relies on the gut's physical attributes rather than any supposed emotional ones: it's long, thin and has some elasticity or stretchiness. A garter was (and sometimes still is) a band tied around the thigh to hold a stocking up, so to threaten to use someone's guts for this purpose means you intend to punish them very severely indeed. The idea goes back at least as far as 1592, when a character in a play by Robert Greene vents his spleen on another by saying, 'I'll make garters of thy guts, thou villain.' Stockings were a normal part of a man's costume in those days, so this wasn't an absurd thing to say in this all-male context.

Venting your spleen brings us to another organ that has emotions associated with it: the spleen was once thought to be the seat of both anger and melancholy. So to vent it was to get rid of these pent-up emotions, particularly the anger. In Shakespeare's *Romeo and Juliet*, an onlooker explains that Romeo tried to break up a fight between Tybalt and Mercutio, but that his gentle words *could not take truce with the unruly spleen/Of Tybalt deaf to peace* – Tybalt, in other words, was spoiling for a fight.

Some of the bodily organs have more gentle associations. Perhaps surprisingly, the bowels are associated with compassion, mercy and other tender feelings – things that we'd nowadays more frequently link to the heart. The epistles of St Paul in the biblical New Testament are fond of this concept: *Put on...bowels of mercies, kindness, humbleness of mind, longsuffering*, he writes to the Colossians and he has similar advice for the Philippians, too. And while we're in odd parts of the body, if your **withers are wrung**, you are tormented, badly upset by something. Humans don't have withers – they're the highest part of a horse's back, between the shoulder blades – but that didn't bother Shakespeare. Hamlet, having asked a troupe of travelling players to perform a certain piece, tells his mother Gertrude that it shouldn't move anyone who doesn't have a guilty conscience: **our withers**, he tells her, **are unwrung**. Gertrude, unfortunately, has a very guilty conscience indeed and her withers are a complete mess.

Any colour you like...

If YELLOW BELLY (page 145) is a racist term, so is *blue-blooded*. It was the Spaniards who initiated this concept, and the English expression is a literal translation of their *sangre azul*, first used in Barbara Hofland's improving story for children *Patience and Perseverance*, published in 1813. The idea was that true Spanish aristocrats had no trace of Moor or other darker-skinned races in their ancestry: their veins showed blue through their pale skins. Hofland's story refers to a grandee, who could easily have been Spanish, but the expression soon spread: only forty years later Elizabeth Gaskell was writing about *the old blue-blooded residents of Cranford*, who were proudly as English as anyone could be.

It's been suggested that being *true blue* is connected with having *blue blood*. It means staunchly loyal, committed to one's principles, qualities that in an earlier time might have been associated with the aristocracy – or at least the aristocrats might have liked to think so. But *true blue* is found in the seventeenth century, well before blue-blooded, and is more likely to be connected with the strength and reliability of blue dye: the old expression *he's true blue and will never stain* suggests a dye that doesn't run when you wash it. When, in the late nineteenth/early twentieth centuries, the British Conservative Party adopted blue as its signature colour (abandoning the traditional red, white and blue of the Union Flag as Labour increasingly laid claim to red), party members were happy to associate themselves with the reliable qualities of a non-staining dye.

Red is, of course, the colour of blood, and the first people *to be caught red-handed* were probably fifteenth-century Scottish poachers, their hands stained by the blood of a stag that had gored them in self-defence. Nowadays you can be caught red-handed without a drop of blood being spilled; you might be robbing a bank or snaffling the last chocolate biscuit – the point is that you've been caught in the act of doing something you shouldn't.

Red-letter days aren't bloodthirsty; they're a cause for celebration. Traditionally (from the seventeenth century) they were holidays or saints' days, printed in red on a calendar where other days were printed in black. By the early nineteenth century, *red-letter days* could be any cause for excitement: the poet Samuel Taylor Coleridge used the expression when he was invited to dine with an author he admired. Today you could apply it to anything from an underdog winning a sporting encounter (*a red-letter day for Bridlington Town*) to a small pleasure that brightens your morning: *It was a red-letter day when the new café opened and I could get a decent cappuccino on my way to work.*

The colour of *a red cent* has no particular symbolism – it simply indicates that the American one-cent coin used to be made from copper. *I haven't a red cent to my name*, *I wouldn't lend her a red cent* and similar expressions refer to this being a tiny sum of money, even though since the 1850s the copper has been mixed with zinc and the reddish hue toned down.

Being **in the pink** inspires more enthusiasm: it means to be in the best of health and spirits, in the best possible condition. This is a reference not so much to the colour as to the small, carnation-like flower. In *Romeo and Juliet* Shakespeare has someone describe himself as *the very pink of courtesy*, meaning the epitome, the best possible example, while a character in *The Wanderer*, by the nineteenth-century novelist Fanny Burney, is *as fresh as a violet, and as fair as jessamy* [jasmine], *and as sweet as a pink*. Pinks were obviously highly thought of.

Although black bile was associated with melancholy and with irritability, if you were bilious your skin was more likely to be a sickly green colour. Thus **green** came to be associated with a variety of emotions, including bad temper and envy. Again, it seems to be Shakespeare who decided that jealousy should be **green-eyed**. Portia in *The Merchant of Venice* gives a list of unpleasant emotions:

> *...doubtful thoughts, and rash-embrac'd despair*
> *And shudd'ring fear, and green-ey'd jealousy...*

…while in *Othello*, the hypocritical, troublemaking Iago warns Othello to beware of jealousy:

> *It is the green-ey'd monster which doth mock*
> *The meat it feeds on –*

…a piece of advice intended to make Othello even more jealous than he already is.

Parallel to this meaning, though, is the one associated with the colour of fresh young plants: transferred to people or ideas, it means naïve, immature, undeveloped. Back to Shakespeare who, in *Antony and Cleopatra*, has Cleopatra refer to her **salad days**, when she was **green in judgement** – in other words, when she was younger and less wise than she is now. Connecting greenness with freshness and innocence goes back several centuries before Shakespeare, but we can be reasonably confident that he invented **salad days**, punning on the young and literally green vegetables that go into a salad.

Green meaning eco-friendly, concerned with the wellbeing of the environment, is much more recent: the Greenpeace movement emerged in Vancouver, Canada, in about 1970, while the German political party whose name translates as Green Action Future was founded in 1978. Both the new meaning of **green** and the campaigns it supported spread rapidly from there.

...so long as it's black

Black, with its connection to darkness and the unknown, has often been used to describe unpleasant, obscure or even evil things: *black magic*, the *black cap* donned by judges to pronounce a sentence of death, to *blackball* someone, declining to let them into a club by placing a black ball rather than a white one into the ballot box.

As far back as the eleventh century, well before it had anything to do with posting a letter, *mail* meant a payment in the form of a tax or a rent. Some five hundred years later, in the Scottish Border country, *black mail* (originally written as two words) was extorted from local farmers by marauding chiefs in return for a promise not to plunder them: what today might be called *protection money*. It took until the nineteenth century for the word to drift into the broader, modern sense of demanding money or favours from someone in order to keep quiet about their guilty secret; the verb *to blackmail* emerged about the same time: *He'd been in trouble as a teenager, so it was easy to blackmail him now that he was a respected public figure.* **Mail** in this sense is of Scandinavian origin; the postal kind and also the *chain mail* worn by knights in armour come from a different French source.

The problem with *a black sheep* is that its wool is difficult to dye – like painting over a dark-coloured wall, it takes a lot more effort (and dye or paint) to produce the effect that you want. So a black sheep is undesirable and even, according to a sixteenth-century ballad, *a perilous beast,* a bad influence on the rest of the flock. In human form, the expression is usually found as *the black sheep of the family*, the one of whom other relatives disapprove, who doesn't have a proper job and who turns up at family gatherings only in the hope of borrowing money.

Speaking of wool, if something is *dyed in the wool* it is dyed before being made up into a garment. This makes the colour faster, more deeply engrained. You might think this sounds like a good thing, but when it's applied to a person (as it has been since Chaucer's time, the late fourteenth century), it takes on a nuance of being stubbornly unchanging, unwilling to listen to other opinions: *He's a dyed-in-the-wool advocate of pen and paper: I've never known him send an email or a text.*

Black can also be used to mean grotesque, darkly humorous, making a joke out of something that isn't normally considered funny: *black comedy* or *black humour.* The term *black humour* was coined by the French surrealist André Breton, who credited the Irish satirist Jonathan Swift with originating the concept. In 1729, Swift published (anonymously, and who can blame him?) an essay called 'A Modest Proposal', which sounds harmless enough until you get to the subtitle: 'For preventing the Children of Poor People From being a Burthen to Their Parents or Country, and For making them Beneficial to the Publick'.

His suggestion was that the Irish poor, frequently encumbered by large families, should sell their spare offspring as food to the rich. Financially advantageous to the poor; of ecological benefit to society; win win. The idea almost caught on: one public figure wrote to Swift suggesting that the policy be extended to England and include not just children but politicians.

Of life and death

You can call this sort of thing **gallows humour**, too: Sigmund Freud wrote an essay about it, suggesting that humour allowed the conscious mind to express thoughts that in serious form would be socially unacceptable. He was writing in German, and some English-language writers continued to use the German **galgenhumor** (of which 'gallows humour' is a direct translation) long after the English version came into common use. People alleged to have made macabre remarks when they are about to be executed include Robert-François Damiens, who was condemned in 1757 for an assassination attempt on the French King Louis XV. Hearing that he was to have his skin burned with hot oil, pitch, wax and sulphur, his body torn apart by four horses and the remains incinerated, he observed, 'Well, it's going to be a tough day.' In 1856, the English murderer Dr William Palmer looked at the trapdoor on the gallows and asked his executioner, 'Are you sure it's safe?'

Allegedly.

The Ancient Romans would have applauded this *sangfroid*. In their day, if a man was condemned for treason, his wife and children might be put to death too and his property confiscated by the state. Suicide was the honourable way out and often entailed *falling on one's sword*. Today you can fall on your sword in a slightly less drastic way, taking the blame for some financial or political crisis by resigning. This is different from becoming a SCAPEGOAT (see page 29): falling on your sword is an admission that something *is* actually your fault.

Speaking of death, there was a time (the fourteenth century) when an *undertaker* was simply a helper; in the sixteenth and beyond it was someone who *undertook* any task or mission, or took on a specified task for a fee. An *undertaker* as an organizer of funerals appeared only around 1700 and competed with the other meanings for well over a hundred years. Then the term *funeral director* emerged, initially in Scotland. For some reason, Americans seem not to have been happy with either of these British options. They got round the problem by deliberately coining the word *mortician* – it was announced in the *Embalmers' Monthly* in February 1895, in response to a request that had appeared in the previous issue. It is presumably adapted from *physician*, someone who deals with the health of the living. As *mors* is the Latin for death, which also gives us *mortal* and *mortuary*, a *mortician* became someone who deals with the dead.

As a matter of interest, the same thing happened in the world of American real estate. The OED cites this announcement in the *National Real Estate Journal* of March 1916:

> *I propose that the National Association adopt a professional title to be conferred upon its members which they shall use to distinguish them from outsiders. That this title be copyrighted and defended by the National Association against misuse... I therefore propose that the National Association adopt and confer upon its members, dealers in realty, the title of realtor.*

The proposal, put forward by one Charles Chadbourn, vice-president of what was then the National Association of Real Estate Boards, was accepted at the association's meeting the following year, and registered American estate agents have been **realtors** ever since.

To revert to death, though, ancient Asian culture provided us with two ways of meeting a sudden and violent one. In the eleventh century members of a breakaway Ismaili sect became notorious for their murders of political and religious opponents: their actions were so uncontrolled that they were known as **Assassins**, a word derived from **hasheesh** and suggesting that the killers were more or less permanently stoned. It took several centuries for the name, without the initial capital, to move into more general use, to denote the killer (often hired) of a prominent figure. In 1606 Shakespeare used *assassination* in *Macbeth* with reference to the murder of King Duncan; in real life one of the first people described as having been *assassinated* was the French King Henri IV, stabbed in Paris by a Catholic fanatic in 1610.

Flourishing in India in the eighteenth and nineteenth centuries, the *Thugs* took their name from a Hindi word for swindler, but their activities were less subtle than that makes them sound. They were devotees of the goddess Kali, but also professional robbers and murderers who strangled their victims in her name. They were suppressed by the British rulers from the 1830s onwards, but their name had by that time been adopted into English to refer to any violent ruffians, whether or not they had a destructive deity egging them on: *Be careful if you are coming home around midnight: there are always lots of thugs about at that hour.*

Death and destruction can be threatened in more delicate ways than this. In the Old Testament Book of Daniel, the Babylonian King Belshazzar is giving a lavish banquet in his palace when a mysterious hand starts writing on the wall in front of him. When all the Babylonian astrologers and wise men fail to interpret the message, the Jewish prisoner Daniel is brought in to see if he can help. Daniel declares that Belshazzar has been *weighed in the balances and found wanting*, and that his great empire is about to fall apart. Which, inevitably, turns out to be true: Belshazzar is slain that very night and Darius the Mede takes over his kingdom.

Today, **the writing on the wall** needn't foretell the fall of a mighty ruler, but it is definitely a warning that some end is in sight: *The writing has been on the wall for the small shops ever since a hypermarket opened on the edge of town.*

Daniel was a useful man in the Babylonian court; he was also called upon to interpret King Nebuchadnezzar's nightmares. We are told that the king had dreamed of a great image:

> *This image's head was of fine gold, his breast and his arms of silver, his belly and his thighs of brass, his legs of iron, his feet part of iron and part of clay.*

Daniel explains that the image represents Nebuchadnezzar's diverse kingdom, the last part of which will be *partly strong and partly broken...even as iron is not mixed with clay.*

There's no need to go into the details of Babylonian history here: they're pretty complex. What matters is that **feet of clay** are a weakness in someone who appears to be made of stronger or better things. Today they are likely to be a moral failing rather than a physical one: *The athlete was shown to have feet of clay when he was caught taking performance-enhancing drugs.*

Still in the Middle East and in the world of the macabre, a **ghoul** was a spirit that stole corpses from the grave and ate them. European travellers discovered this legend in the eighteenth century and by the mid-nineteenth the novelist William Makepeace Thackeray was writing about *ghouls feasting on the fresh corpse of a reputation*. That's very much the sense that the word has now: someone taking a morbid delight in unpleasant things, whether it be malicious gossip or gory horror films.

The police are probably responsible for **the graveyard shift**, although it occurs in gambling circles and in the navy as well – all from the late nineteenth and early twentieth century. There's no evidence to link the expression to graveyards, or to people standing watch over them to guard against graverobbing: it simply means the shift between (usually) midnight and eight in the morning, though on board ship **the graveyard watch** was between midnight and 4 a.m. One explanation for the latter is that a lot of disasters – hitting icebergs or having people fall overboard – occurred during that time; on dry land it was more likely to mean that nothing much happened at all – that everything was **as silent as the grave**.

The original **kiss of death** didn't kill anyone directly, but it did lead to their death. It comes from the New Testament story of Judas kissing Jesus in order to identify him to the authorities, leading to his arrest and subsequent crucifixion. Despite what Shirley Bassey sings in the theme song of the James Bond film *Goldfinger*, the villainous Mr Goldfinger doesn't administer a literal **kiss of death**: he covers his victim with gold paint, leading to 'skin suffocation'. Away from both the Bible and the world of espionage, *a kiss of death* doesn't have to involve a kiss – it can be any action, often apparently innocent or arbitrary, that leads to disaster: *The warm winter meant there was no skiing: it was the kiss of death to the resort hotels.*

In ancient Jewish temples a veil separated the inner sanctuary (known as the **holy of holies**) from the outer part, metaphorically separating God from humanity; a similar concept exists in some Christian churches. To pass **beyond the veil,** therefore, is to join God, to die. **To give up the ghost** is another Christian way of phrasing it, allowing the Holy Ghost or Holy Spirit to pass out of your body. You don't have to die **to give up the ghost**, though – you don't even have to be a living being: *The bus gave up the ghost on the steep hill: all the passengers had to get out and push.*

At death's door is another variation on this theme, found in an eleventh-century psalter (book of psalms) and frequently in later texts. It means extremely ill and is often used in a rather melodramatic style: *You may say it's only a cold, but I've been at death's door for a week.*

Another metaphor for dying sounds as if it comes from the Wild West, but **to bite the dust** or, in an earlier form, **to bite the ground**, is much older than that: the poet John Dryden used it in his 1697 translation of Virgil's *Aeneid* (written in Latin in the first century BC). There, it refers to the many dead in battles between various Italian tribes before the founding of Rome. Although cowboys in old westerns always seemed to fall artistically from horses, and horses were certainly used in warfare in the *Aeneid*, **biting the dust** doesn't insist on this: it simply means that the dead are lying face down. Today it's likely to be a project or an idea rather than a person that bites the dust: *Our wedding plans bit the dust when we discovered that the venue we wanted was booked for two years ahead.*

Projects and ideas are the theme of the final chapter. Time to get ourselves **galvanized into action.**

CHAPTER 8

The Tower of Babel and Seventh Heaven

We can often learn about where things come from by taking a closer look at what we call them. The names of fabrics are particularly apt to betray their roots. *Calico* originated in Calicut in India, *damask* in Damascus in Syria and *cambric* in Cambrai in France. *Denim* was French, too: as early as the seventeenth century *serge de Nîmes* was a woollen fabric from the town of Nîmes, and by 1864 Webster's *American Dictionary of the English Language* had dropped the *serge* and adopted the modern spelling. By this time denim was being used to make *jeans*, although for several centuries before that *jean* had been the name of a cloth that may have been first produced in the Italian city of *Genoa*. And while *suede* has a French name it started out in Sweden and was used to make what were known as Swedish gloves or, in French, *gants de Suède*.

What's in a name?

We use even more words derived from the names of inventors, from the French acrobat Jules **Léotard**, who popularized a one-piece, body-hugging garment, to the Duke of **Wellington**, who instructed his shoemaker to redesign the prevailing fashion for Hessian boots and make something both hard-wearing and smart. An eighteenth-century French finance minister, Étienne de **Silhouette**, was so notoriously tight-fisted that his name was borrowed for anything done on the cheap, specifically a sort of portrait showing nothing more than its subject's outline in black card. Another Frenchman, a physician called Joseph-Ignace **Guillotin,** was the instigator, if not the inventor, of the method of execution that bears his name, though to be fair to him he suggested it as being quicker and therefore more humane than hanging.

When we talk about *galvanizing someone into action* – spurring them on, encouraging them to get on with something – we're referring to the technology that inspired Mary Shelley to write *Frankenstein* in 1816. Luigi **Galvani** was an eighteenth-century Italian scientist who, probably accidentally, discovered that if you put an electric charge through the leg of a dead frog, the muscles contracted and it appeared to come back to life. His experiments on 'animal electricity' – electricity as an intrinsic force in living creatures, flowing through their bodies as easily as blood – gave Shelley the idea of animating what she called the Creature, now better known from film versions of her story as Frankenstein's monster.

Why Galvani's name was also adopted for *galvanization* – covering iron or steel with a coating of zinc to protect rusting – is unclear, as much of the development of this process was done by a near-contemporary, Alessandro *Volta*, who gave his name to the early battery known as the *voltaic pile*, and to the *volt*, the SI unit of electric potential. The names of scientific units of measurement frequently commemorate their discoverers: the *amp* (from *ampere*), the *hertz*, the *ohm* and the *kelvin* are all named after scientists who made significant contributions to their fields. So are the *faraday*, the *siemens*, the *coulomb* and the *lambert*, not to mention the temperature scales *Celsius*, *Fahrenheit* and *Réaumur*. Almost all these scientists were, of course, male: there's very little evidence of women's contribution until Marie Curie came along and had an element (*curium*) named after her and another (*polonium*) after her country of origin. In the early days male domination was so absolute that even the distinctly female *Fallopian tubes* recall the work of a man – a sixteenth-century Italian physician and priest called Gabriele Falloppio (or, in Latin, *Fallopius*, hence the single *p* in the anatomical name).

The source of these eponyms is usually obvious – if you're going to name something after yourself or your patron, why be coy? Better hidden than most is John McAdam, the Scottish engineer who, around 1820, pioneered a method of road construction known as **macadamization**. This involved compacting layer upon layer of broken stones to form a smooth, hard surface. It was a great improvement on what had gone before, but unfortunately vehicles driving over it raised a lot of dust and gradually destroyed it. These issues were addressed some eighty years later and many decades after McAdam's death by spraying the stones with tar to produce what is to this day known as **tarmac**, abbreviated from **tarmacadam**.

An unpleasant aside: levelling the surface of a road in preparation for tarmacking might, since the 1930s, be done by a **bulldozer**. Before this heavyweight form of tractor was invented, a **bulldozer** was a person who used their strength to intimidate and to get their own way. It comes from the idea, in use in the United States in the nineteenth century, of administering **a bull dose** – a dose large enough to deal with a bull. This might refer to a dose of medicine, but was equally likely to be a punishment meted out to a disobedient slave, a thrashing that brought him close to death.

One scientific process owes its name to a patron of a much earlier date: *vulcanization*, the action of hardening rubber by exposing it to sulphur, derives from Vulcan, the Roman god of fire and metalworking. According to tradition, Vulcan's smithy was situated beneath Mount Etna in Sicily (the word *volcano* also derives from his name). So Vulcan has always been closely linked to both heat and sulphur, even if no one is claiming that he actually came up with the vulcanization process. Credit for that lies with Thomas Hancock, an English inventor who patented it in 1843.

While we're in the realm of Classical mythology, a man called Tantalus offended the gods (an easy thing to do) and was condemned to spend eternity up to his waist in water which receded whenever he bent down to try to drink. Trees laden with fruit dangled above his head, their branches drawing back whenever he reached up to them. It's from this tortured soul that we get the word *tantalize*, to tease or torment with things that remain literally or figuratively beyond your grasp: *I had a tantalizing glimpse of wealth and fame before I failed my music exam.* There's also an agonizing nineteenth-century invention called a *tantalus*, a device containing decanters whose alcoholic contents are in plain view but can't be accessed if you don't know how the mechanism works. The tantalus has an odd claim to fame: it was invented by a Dutch cabinet maker called George Betjeman, grandfather of the future Poet Laureate John Betjeman, who described it as 'the source of the family fortune'. George was obviously a modest man: most people in his position would have named the device a *betjeman*.

Modesty doesn't seem to have carried the same weight with the British army officer who, in the late eighteenth century, invented a hollow projectile that contained both bullets and explosive. When detonated, the explosive burst the shell and showered the ammunition in all directions. The officer in question was a Major Henry *Shrapnel*.

Some building work

The term *jerry-built* is too old to be an insulting reference to German workmanship: *Jerry* as a slang term for a German soldier didn't appear until the First World War, by which time the idea of *jerry-building* – building houses as quickly as possible with little regard for quality of materials or workmanship – had been around for at least forty years. There are stories of a Liverpool firm of builders called Jerry Brothers, who might have been to blame, but there's no hard evidence. An alternative suggestion that Jerry is short for Jericho and that the idiom derives from the Old Testament story (told in the Book of Joshua) of the walls of the city of Jericho falling down when the Israelite priests blew their trumpets doesn't seem to be true either. Pity, because as an example of jerry-building, walls that fell down when someone blew a trumpet too close to them would be hard to beat.

Continuing with the digression into biblical buildings, after the flood mentioned in Chapter 3 (see page 51), the descendants of Noah went out and populated the world. At that time everyone the world over spoke the same language and they took it into their heads to build a city with a tower that would reach Heaven. This woke God up to the idea that people who could communicate easily could do anything they set their minds to; they could even challenge His supremacy, which hadn't been part of His plan when He created us. So he decided to *confound their language, that they may not understand one another's speech*, inventing different languages and putting an end to international co-operation. The Bible doesn't tell us what happened to the tower – God scattered the people across the face of the earth before they could complete it. But we do know that the city was called Babel, from a Hebrew word for confusion. By the sixteenth century, **babel** had come to mean a disorderly muddle of sounds, an incomprehensible din: *Before the meeting started I could hear a babel of voices: we were obviously in for a heated discussion.*

The term **Tower of Babel** doesn't appear in the Bible, but it can be used to describe any overly ambitious project that is doomed to failure. The **Babel fish** – a device that translates instantly from any language to any other, which features in Douglas Adams' *A Hitchhiker's Guide to the Galaxy* (first broadcast on radio in 1978 and appearing in book form in 1979) – also takes its name from this story, because of course Arthur Dent and friends wouldn't have needed a Babel fish had

God not invented all those languages way back in the Book of Genesis. It's a tribute to Adams, rather than to those ambitious builders of biblical times, that a multilingual translation app launched by Yahoo at the end of the last century was also called Babel Fish.

Still loosely in the field of building, there may not be many words that come to us from surveying, but there is at least one. Back in the day (from the early nineteenth century or so) surveyors would carve a special *mark* – a broad arrow with a horizontal bar across it – into a rock or some other solid substance, at a point whose exact elevation and position they knew. Into this mark they could insert an angle-iron, which served as a ***bench*** to support a levelling-staff and calculate the elevation and position of other points. Never mind if you can't follow the technicalities; what's important here is that, once one surveyor had moved on, another could come along, insert their own angle-iron and make their own calculations, knowing that they were starting from the same assumptions, the same fixed point – the same ***benchmark*** – as their colleague. Non-surveyors were soon using the word to mean any known point or 'given' against which others can be measured: *The academy's results were a benchmark for assessing the performance of other local schools.*

Monty or Burton? Or both?

Reverting to the England of the early twentieth century – we were there with *jerry-building* a few pages ago, if you remember – Sir Montague Maurice Burton founded the gentleman's tailoring stores that bear his name, opening his first shop in Chesterfield, Derbyshire, in 1903, and quickly expanding nationwide. There are many who believe that *the full monty* originally referred to customers ordering a three-piece suit – the whole lot, the works – from one of Burton's establishments. Others maintain that it's to do with the World War Two hero Field Marshal Bernard Montgomery wearing an impressive chestful of medals on ceremonial occasions (see TOP BRASS on page 15). But the expression didn't emerge until the 1970s, by which time both Montague Burton and the Field Marshal had died, so neither of these explanations is entirely convincing. What isn't in doubt, though, is that it gained wide popularity with the 1997 film *The Full Monty*, in which a group of unemployed men-turned-strippers decide to give their audience *the full monty* by removing even their posing pouches. A long way from a three-piece suit.

As for *gone for a Burton*, old RAF slang for being dead or, in the case of a plan, ruined, there's no linking that to Sir Monty. It's more likely to be a reference to the town of Burton-on-Trent in Staffordshire, famed for its beer: a pilot who was missing from his quarters because he had been killed in action might euphemistically have been said to have gone out for a drink.

Tom, Dick, Harry and the rest

Moving from individual names to more generic ones, *every Tom, Dick or Harry* means all the ordinary people – probably because in medieval times Tom, Dick and Harry were names given to ordinary folk, while their aristocratic equivalents insisted on the respect attached to Thomas, Richard and Henry. Tom in particular was once widely used to represent a certain type of person: *Tom Fool*, for example, was the archetype of a foolish person, so his activities became *tomfoolery*. A *Tom of all trade*s was, in the seventeenth century, someone who was quite good at all sorts of things but not brilliant at any of them. By the eighteenth century he had become a *Jack of all trades, and master of none*, *Jack* being another of those all-purpose names that crops up in expressions such as *Jack Tar,* an ordinary sailor; *Jack in office*, someone who is petty and officious about doing their job; *Jack the lad*, a brash and overly confident young man; the children's toy a *jack-in-the-box*; and the *Jack-o'-lantern* carved out of a pumpkin at Hallowe'en. If you flip back to Chapter 5 you'll find similar concepts in the use of Robin and Jenny (page 92).

How does your garden grow?

We seem to have strayed a long way from people naming things after themselves. But there are many more examples. The plant hunters, primarily of the eighteenth and nineteenth centuries, were another gang who put their names to anything they could conceivably lay claim to. Or if not their own names, those of their employers or sponsors. Perhaps most obviously the *Douglas fir* is named after David Douglas, a Scottish gardener who did his training at the Palace of Scone and later worked at Glasgow Botanic Gardens. The Douglas fir's botanical name is *Pseudotsuga menziesii*, in honour of Archibald Menzies, another Scot, who might have become better known had his plant-hunting zeal not been held in check by the captain of the ship on which he travelled, George Vancouver, commemorated in the name of the Canadian city. *Pseudotsuga*, by the way, means it's a false hemlock, but that is taking us into deep botanical waters.

Forsythia is named after William Forsyth, Superintendent of Royal Gardens at Kensington Palace in Victorian times; *banksia* after Joseph Banks, who accompanied James Cook on his first voyage to the South Pacific and returned to be an adviser at Kew; *mahonia* after Bernard M'Mahon, who travelled in North America on the great Lewis and Clark expedition of 1803–6; *magnolia* after Pierre Magnol, seventeenth-century director of the botanic gardens in Montpellier. This is a list that could go on and on.

The man sometimes regarded as Australia's first natural historian, the seventeenth- and eighteenth-century explorer (some say pirate) William Dampier, has a genus of Australian shrubs, *Dampiera*, named after him, not to mention several geographical features and settlements in Oceania, and a minor planet. But he is also responsible for introducing a much more familiar word. His 1697 journal *A New Voyage Around the World* has the first recorded use of **barbecue**, not as a grill for cooking but as a framework of sticks for sleeping on. Set about a metre above the ground, it was designed to protect the sleeper from rats and other marauding creatures. Within a few decades the word had come to mean an animal roasted whole on a similar grill, or a large social gathering centred round it – what we might today call a hog roast. One of the first people who recorded having attended such a gathering, in 1769, was an up-and-coming politician called George Washington. Perhaps surprisingly after this promising start, the smaller-scale barbecue, the kind you might have in your own back garden, didn't become popular until the 1930s.

The well-travelled Dampier, by the way, also gave us the first recorded use of **avocado** (which he observed on the island of Chepelio, off the coast of Panama) and **chopsticks** (in what is now Vietnam).

Wherever you found your plants, cultivating the soil used to be hard work. Until farming started to be mechanized in the eighteenth century, much of the labour was done by hand and an old word for tilling the soil by hand was **manure**. It's related to **manoeuvre**, both words being derived from the French for **hand** and **work**. John Milton's *Paradise Lost*, first published in 1667, refers to *flowery arbours…*

> *…with branches overgrown,*
> *That mock our scant manuring, and require*
> *More hands than ours to lop*
> *their wanton growth.*

In other words, they're growing like mad and we don't have the workforce to control them. The old meaning and the new had existed side by side for a century before *Paradise Lost*: **manure** had become a noun meaning fertilizer by the 1530s and a verb meaning to apply manure by 1577. It was probably still hard work, though.

How high the moon?

In a largely agricultural world, the seasons and the weather were obviously important, dictating when to plant or harvest and bringing with them omens of good or bad fortune (one of the most famous, the idea that a **red sky at night** brings good weather – **a shepherd's** or **sailor's delight** – is found in a translation of the Bible as early as 1395). The phases of the moon played their part, too. There are two sorts of **blue moon**, only one of them actually blue. Well, not really blue, just *looking* blue, because you are seeing it through dust particles, probably the aftermath of a volcanic eruption. This doesn't happen often, but when it does it can be quite spectacular: after the volcano Krakatoa erupted in Indonesia in 1883, the moon looked blue for two years, even if you were viewing it from as far afield as Europe or America. By that time the expression **once in a blue moon**, meaning very rarely indeed, had been around for half a century, but that distant and destructive eruption doubtless gave it extra clout.

The non-blue kind of blue moon is more frequent, sometimes appearing as often as twice a year (so not really **once in a blue moon** at all). It is an extra full moon occurring in a given period: either a second one within a calendar month or a fourth one in three months. Unless it's February, a calendar month is longer than a lunar month, which averages around twenty-nine and a half days, so it's easy for the moon to slip in an additional full phase every now and then.

Going back to the dust particles, they make the moon look blue only if the vast majority of them are wider than the wavelength of red light (0.7 micrometres). Smaller than that, or a mixture of sizes, and you'll get a red moon, which is more common and understandably hasn't given rise to an idiom to do with rarity.

You don't need dust particles to obscure the moon, of course. Everyday clouds will do the job just as well. They can obscure reality, too. *To have your head in the clouds* is to be impractical, to be dreaming about something that isn't going to happen and ignoring any difficulties in the way. We owe the similar idea of *being in cloud-cuckoo-land* to the Ancient Greek playwright Aristophanes, in whose comedy *The Birds* the birds build a kingdom that separates humanity from the gods and will in theory give the birds power over both. The name has come to mean any unrealistic state of affairs that is the result of wishful thinking: *He's living in cloud-cuckoo-land if he thinks the election will change anything.*

Then there are *cloud nine* and *seventh heaven*, both places where you can be in ecstasy, in a state of unmitigated delight. Three, seven and nine are lucky numbers in many cultures and contexts: in Judaic and Christian culture the emphasis on seven may be because God created the world in six days and rested on the seventh. Whatever the reason, its influence extends from the seven deadly sins to the supposed luck inherited by the seventh son of a seventh son. Both Judaism and Islam once believed that there were seven heavens (each ruled by a different planet) and that the seventh was the highest, the best, the one where God resided or where His divine light shone. So in both a secular and a religious sense, *the seventh heaven* came to signify the best possible place to be. Oddly enough, early Christians only counted up to three heavens: St Paul, writing to the Corinthians, tells his readers that he knew a man who was *caught up to the third heaven…caught up into paradise and heard unspeakable words, which it is not lawful for a man to utter.* Same concept, just four layers closer.

All this may explain why an alternative (largely American) version of **on cloud nine** is **on cloud seven**: it may simply be that anything to do with seven is likely to be a good thing. So why did **cloud nine** become more popular? No one is sure. Most modern meteorologists distinguish ten major types of cloud but divide them into only three layers – low-level, middle and high-level. Nothing very euphoric about that. Best guess about cloud nine seems to give credit to a 1950s American radio show called *Yours Truly, Johnny Dollar,* about an insurance investigator who frequently manages to get himself knocked unconscious and, on waking up, always claims to have been in a blissful place he calls cloud nine. Perhaps he was just going that little bit better than the established **cloud seven**. A few years later, Sam Ross, a writer of hard-boiled thrillers, went further still when he wrote *That stuff is way up on Cloud Thirty-Nine*; shortly after that the jazz magazine *Down Beat* was saying *I don't like strange music, I'm not on Cloud Nine.* Then in 1969 the Motown group The Temptations had a hit with a song called 'Cloud Nine', in which the singer 'takes to cloud nine' to escape the horrors of his home life; the chorus tells us that on cloud nine you're 'a million miles from reality'. Johnny Dollar might have got there thanks to a blow to the head; as we make our way through the 1960s it's hard not to detect a whiff of mind-altering substances.

The idea that nine is a symbol of perfection, or at least of something special, may be the explanation of *being dressed (up) to the nines*. From the eighteenth century onwards *to the nines* meant to the highest degree, to a great standard of excellence. You could be *pleased to the nines* if you were absolutely delighted, or *reproduce something to the nines* if you did it very accurately. The idea of being dressed to the nines evolved naturally from this: there's no convincing evidence for the suggestion that a certain 99th regiment was always so smartly turned out that every other army division tried to emulate it. It's a nice image, but surely you'd have said *dressed up to the ninety-nines* if that was what you meant.

Thunderbolts and lightning

A weather phenomenon we might greet with less enthusiasm than cloud nine is a *perfect storm*, a particularly violent storm produced when a number of different conditions (heavy rains, high winds and low temperatures, for example) occur at the same time. Metaphorically – and only since the 1990s

– a **perfect storm** is a complete catastrophe, again caused by a combination of events that would be bad enough if they occurred separately: *The global crash, low interest rates and the raising of their pensionable age created a perfect storm financially for anyone born in the 1950s.*

Stealing someone's thunder – taking credit for something they have done or diverting attention from their achievements – is connected not to the weather but to the theatre. The story goes that one John Dennis, largely forgotten except for this anecdote, wrote a play called *Appius and Virginia* in which he needed to create the effect of a thunderstorm; he came up with the idea of rattling a sheet of tin. The play, performed at Drury Lane in London in 1709, was not a success and the management quickly withdrew it. However, Dennis subsequently attended a performance of *Macbeth* in which the various storms were created using his technique. Deeply incensed, he cried out, 'They will not let my play run, and yet they steal my thunder!' The expression can now be used to cover any set of circumstances in which someone is overshadowed, usually unjustly: *She stole my thunder by presenting my report as if she had done the work.*

Another image that we owe to the theatre is to do with lime – not the fruit, but the mineral calcium oxide. This burns very brightly if you heat it with a mixture of oxygen and hydrogen.

Not only that, but it gives off little heat, a useful attribute in a crowded theatre that is likely to be quite warm enough already. That's what the Scottish engineer Thomas Drummond discovered in the 1820s. **Lime light** – originally two words, now usually one – became a popular way of illuminating a scene or a leading actor, directing attention towards whatever was most important on the stage. **To be in the limelight**, therefore, came to mean to be the focus of attention, to be in the glare of publicity. This may or may not be a good thing, though if you **steal the limelight** it's likely to be deliberate: *She stole the limelight by wearing a bright red dress when everyone else was in black.*

Still in the theatre, it's a style of Spanish melodrama that gives us **cloak and dagger**, though both the Spaniards and the French called it 'cloak and sword'. In plays of this genre, popular in the eighteenth and nineteenth centuries, the principal characters would have worn a cloak and concealed their weapon under it. The expression was well enough known in English in 1841 for Charles Dickens to use it in *Barnaby Rudge*: a servant brings his master a note that reads 'A friend. Desiring of a conference. Immediate. Private. Burn it when you've read it.' The servant explains that it was given to him by a man waiting at the door. 'With a cloak and dagger?' suggests the master, implying that his unknown correspondent has an unnecessarily theatrical approach to note-writing. Modern usage has strayed away from the melodramatic and into the clandestine, the world of secrecy and plotting: *There's lots of cloak-and-dagger negotiation going on, but sooner or later they'll have to issue a statement.*

News travels...

The invention of the telegraph in the nineteenth century improved the delivery of messages, whether or not they were cloak and dagger in nature. They could now go directly from one place to another down the newly installed wires, arriving at their destination with speed and accuracy. There are several stories to account for less reliable methods of transmission being described as **through the grapevine**. One tells of an 1850s entrepreneur, eager to cash in on the new technology, who attempted to string a telegraph wire between existing trees rather than going to the trouble of erecting purpose-built poles. The movement of the trees made the wires fall in a writhing heap on the ground, similar to the tendrils of a grapevine. Alternatively, the grapevine analogy may refer to the circuitous route of passing a story along by word of mouth. Funk and Wagnall's late-nineteenth-century *Standard Dictionary of the English Language* (an American publication) says that **grapevine** is short for **a despatch by grape-vine telegraph**, so that the grapevine was not the means of transmission but the result – a rumour or unsubstantiated piece of news. It wasn't long after that that **I heard it through** *the grapevine* came to mean what it means today: 'I heard it from a source I don't know or don't choose to name; it may or may not be reliable information.'

And so we come *full circle* – another expression for which we can thank Shakespeare. He used it in *King Lear*, first performed in 1606. As we saw in the introduction, our understanding of where words and expressions come from does sometimes depend on information that isn't entirely reliable. But, *when the chips are down*, there's often a good story to tell anyway and that surely makes it all *fair game*.

References

Cresswell, Julia, *The Cat's Pyjamas* (Penguin, 2007)

Engel, Matthew, *That's the Way It Crumbles* (Profile, 2017)

Flavell, Linda and Roger, *Dictionary of Idioms and Their Origins* (Kyle Cathie, 1992)

—*Dictionary of Word Origins* (Kyle Cathie, 1993)

—*Dictionary of English Down the Ages* (Kyle Cathie, 2005)

Moore, John, *You English Words* (Collins, 1961)

Parkinson, Judy, *Spilling the Beans on the Cat's Pyjamas* (Michael O'Mara, 2009)

Taggart, Caroline, *Pushing the Envelope* (Michael O'Mara, 2011)

—*As Right As Rain* (Michael O'Mara, 2013)

The Phrase Finder (www.phrases.org.uk) is a wonderful resource for anyone interested in this subject, giving the origins of 2000 idioms, phrases and proverbs.

The background to cupboards given in Chapter 1 came from an Arts Society lecture by Janusz Karczewski-Slowikowski. The explanation for *paying out* in an 1898 edition of *Notes and Queries* discussed in Chapter 5 was quoted by Professor Anatoly Liberman in his column 'The Oxford Etymologist' (blog.oup.com). The sixteenth-century ballad mentioned in Chapter 7 with reference to black sheep is quoted in Linda and Roger Flavell's *Dictionary of Idioms*.

Index